Ch'ixinakax utxiwa

T0056399

Critical South

The publication of this series is supported by the International Consortium of Critical Theory Programs funded by the Andrew W. Mellon Foundation.

Series editors: Natalia Brizuela and Leticia Sabsay

Ch'ixinakax utxiwa

On Practices and Discourses of Decolonization

Silvia Rivera Cusicanqui

Translated by Molly Geidel

polity

First published as *Ch'ixinakax utxiwa. Una reflexión sobre prácticas y discursos descolonizadores* by Tinta Limón Ediciones, Buenos Aires, 2010
© 2010, Silvia Rivera Cusicanqui. Published by agreement of Tina Limón Ediciones.

This English edition © 2020 by Polity Press

Silvia Rivera Cusicanqui, "*Ch'ixinakax utxiwa*: A Reflection on the Practices and Discourses of Decolonization," in *South Atlantic Quarterly*, Volume 111, no. 1, pp. 95–109. Copyright, 2012, Duke University Press. All rights reserved. Republished by permission of the copyright holder, Duke University Press. www.dukeupress.edu

A revised translation of Chapter 1, "Another Bicentennial," has been included in this work by kind permission of *emisférica*, the online journal of the Hemispheric Institute of Performance and Politics

Polity Press
65 Bridge Street
Cambridge CB2 1UR, UK

Polity Press
101 Station Landing
Suite 300
Medford, MA 02155, USA

All rights reserved. Except for the quotation of short passages for the purpose of criticism and review, no part of this publication may be reproduced, stored in a retrieval system or transmitted, in any form or by any means, electronic, mechanical, photocopying, recording or otherwise, without the prior permission of the publisher.

ISBN-13: 978-1-5095-3782-2 – hardback
ISBN-13: 978-1-5095-3783-9 – paperback

A catalogue record for this book is available from the British Library.

Library of Congress Cataloging-in-Publication Data

Names: Rivera Cusicanqui, Silvia, author. | Geidel, Molly, translator.
Title: Ch'ixinakax utxiwa : on practices and discourses of decolonisation / Silvia Rivera Cusicanqui ; translated by Molly Geidel.
Other titles: Ch'ixinakax utxiwa. English
Description: Cambridge, UK ; Medford, MA : Polity, 2020. | Series: Critical South | Includes bibliographical references and index. | Summary: "A cutting-edge work on how colonial structures of domination affect indigenous identities and cultures"-- Provided by publisher.
Identifiers: LCCN 2020001426 | ISBN 9781509537822 (hardback) | ISBN 9781509537839 (paperback)
Subjects: LCSH: Decolonization. | Indians of South America.
Classification: LCC JV185 .R5613 2020 | DDC 980/.00498--dc23
LC record available at https://lccn.loc.gov/2020001426

Typeset in 12.5 on 17pt Sabon
by Fakenham Prepress Solutions, Fakenham, Norfolk NR21 8NL
Printed and bound in Great Britain by TJ International Limited

The publisher has used its best endeavours to ensure that the URLs for external websites referred to in this book are correct and active at the time of going to press. However, the publisher has no responsibility for the websites and can make no guarantee that a site will remain live or that the content is or will remain appropriate.

Every effort has been made to trace all copyright holders, but if any have been overlooked the publisher will be pleased to include any necessary credits in any subsequent reprint or edition.

For further information on Polity, visit our website:
politybooks.com

Contents

Publisher's Note

The Introduction and chapters 1 and 2 were translated by Molly Geidel. Chapter 3 was translated by Brenda Baletti and is reproduced here by permission of Duke University Press.

Introduction: The Silvia Rivera Cusicanqui Principle: The Rebellion of Thought

Véronica Gago

Reading Lenin as one reads the *I Ching*, opening to a random page and discovering the phrase: "We must dream, on the condition that we believe in our dreams, that we day-by-day compare them to reality, that we meticulously realize our fantasy."[1] Silvia Rivera Cusicanqui recounts how this citation saved her from the disapproval of a thesis panel that insisted on testing for a theoretical purity her work did not contain. It was the 1970s and she was getting a sociology degree, thus nobody could object to Lenin, and at the same time finding Lenin speaking of fantasy was a discovery to treasure.

In this scene we can see a distillation of Silvia's worldview: an intellectual passion for political struggles, a political passion for irreverent intellectual craftsmanship, and a mistrust of canonical objects. Silvia Rivera Cusicanqui is one of the most lucid, inventive, and galvanizing intellectuals on our continent. Her mode of *doing* knowledge and *practicing* theory allows us to read in her work a permanent state of rebellion, indispensable for thinking in times of retreats and losses, crises and reversals.

The anticolonial key: reading Frantz Fanon through Fausto Reinaga

That thesis, with the crowning quote by a Lenin speaking of fantasy, was lost when the military government raided Silvia's house in the city of La Paz. Later she went into exile in Buenos Aires, while pregnant with her first child and after being imprisoned for her political militancy. But she didn't stay long in Argentina: she worked conducting social surveys, and people barely responded to her. "It was like I was invisible," she remembers of the racism she encountered. She departed for the north of Argentina and felt more at home there, picking up an enduring knowledge of smuggling and the custom of not buying furniture but instead making it out of bricks and boards that can be easily dismantled.

The period of military governments in Bolivia spanned between 1964 and 1982, and ended thanks to popular resistance under the strong leadership of the Bolivian Workers' Center (COB) and the Unified Syndical Confederation of Rural Workers of Bolivia (CSUTCB). During those clamorous years, Silvia wrote what would become a classic work: *Oppressed but not Defeated: Peasant Struggles Among the Aymara and Quechwa in Bolivia, 1900–1980,*[2] which shows the "logic of rebellion" that guided all the uprisings of this period, up until the coup by Luis García Meza in July 1980 (which toppled Lidia Gueiler, the interim constitutional president, a few days before Hernán Siles Zuazo would have returned to power after winning in the presidential polls).

Oppressed but not Defeated, whose title already announces a political thesis, was informed by Silvia's experience in the countryside. There she was involved with *katarismo*, the *indigenista* guerrilla movement of the 1960s and 1970s that embodied a collective moment of political radicalization. One of her key intellectual influences, Fausto Reinaga (1906–1994), forcefully introduced in his 1969 book *La revolución india* his reading of Frantz Fanon, constructing a powerful analogy between the Black and Indian situation (with all the ambivalence contained in those categories). As Gustavo Cruz has commented, "there is a Fanonist/Reinaguist critique of the imitation of the Western or European model" which already by that moment had "gained epistemic and political centrality."[3] Reinaga, in open discussion with nationalism and Marxism, registers "an encounter between Black power and Indian power in one of the Souths of the West," concludes Cruz.[4] In that atmosphere Silvia wrote *Oppressed but not Defeated*, which allows readers to *listen* to almost a century of worker–peasant alliances in an Indian key, as a plot of resistance and as a long memory which functions as anticolonial practice at the heart of the popular. The book was first published by a La Paz press and the CSUTCB, in a gesture of claiming the book on the part of that peasant organization; later, according to the author, the book would become part of a project of "reformist appropriation by the intellectuals of the 'pluri-multi' generation," which demonstrated "the elites' rhetorical capacities, and their enormous flexibility in channeling their collective guilt into touch-ups on the façade of the matrix of domination, thus renewing its colonial dimension."[5]

Subsequently, this research in the service of decolonizing thought and history branched off into the Andean Oral History Workshop (THOA), which Silvia cofounded in the early 1980s. An original collective intellectual undertaking, THOA explored the communitarian and anarchist aspects of popular struggle and disseminated their research through pamphlets and radio plays, succeeding in influencing the popular movements of the following years, especially in the organization of the ayllus[6] of Western Bolivia, the National Council of Ayllus and Markas of Qullasuyu (CONAMAQ). From this work of interviews, workshops, and encounters, Silvia and Zulema Lehm compiled *Los artesanos libertarios y la ética del trabajo* (published in 1988; republished by Tinta Limón and Madre Selva in 2014). The book chronicles the history of unions in the 1920s before the Chaco War between Bolivia and Paraguay, but also after the bloodshed (in which more than 100,000 lives were lost from both sides), charting the growing importance of the women's unions of florists, cooks, and market vendors. The book's history reaches the 1950s but, according to the authors, "sometimes takes zigzagging or diffuse paths" to reconstruct the memory of the worker–artisan movement and its organizational development with a strong stamp of women's leadership. Once more, Silvia's work provides a variation on the theme of not being defeated; libertarianism understood in an anticolonial key; the oral narration that makes possible the persistence of struggle; and the memory that transforms history into a place "full of now-time," as Walter Benjamin said in his famous theses.

Of migrant routes and borders

Rivera Cusicanqui has an art, and that is escaping classification, particularly the exoticizing categories in which many want to place her. She says for this reason people often think she's an anthropologist. She laughs and baptizes herself an "unidentified ethnic object." Sometimes, too, she refers to herself as a *sochóloga*, a mixture of *chola*[7] and sociologist that was once used to discredit her and which she now wears as a badge of honor. In the same way, she plays with the term *birchola*, a mix of *chola*, a woman dressed in the pleated skirt (*pollera*) that marks urban indigenous identity, and *birlocha*, which was how, in contrast, women in "modern" dress were denoted; Silvia researched these figures among the migrants of the populous city of El Alto, the urban periphery that surrounds La Paz. These are not simply clever word games. They are flashes of a deeper humor, and of a ruthless critique of the tendency to essentialize indigeneity.

Bircholas: trabajo de mujeres. Explotación capitalista y opresión colonial entre las migrantes aymaras de La Paz y El Alto[8] is the next landmark work in Silvia's oeuvre I want to emphasize. Published at the beginning of the new century, it is an important study of the migration routes of women who create communal territory in the midst of colonial oppression and capitalist exploitation. One year later, Silvia would trace these migration trajectories from the perspective of the coca leaf in *Las fronteras de la coca: epistemologías coloniales y circuitos alternativos de la hoja de coca. El caso de la frontera boliviano–argentina.*[9] These two circuits connect, and they share a border epistemology: in *Las fronteras* Silvia again mixes temporalities, reading border spaces as problematic objects and tracing the journey of the coca leaf that challenged colonial markets. A global force for the decriminalization of coca, Silvia also cultivates her own coca harvest, propagates a coca-infused cuisine (crepes, cakes, and energizing smoothies), and strengthens networks of coca cultivation for legal use. She developed this campaign as part of Evo Morales' government, where she briefly held a position. She later became a radical critic of the MAS government, as summarized by the title of a book she wrote, *Mito y desarrollo en Bolivia. El giro colonial del gobierno del MAS* (i.e. *Myth and Development in Bolivia. The Colonial Turn of the MAS Government*).[10]

Silvia's work cannot be understood without understanding the spiraled time, or, more precisely, the layered time, in which these routes and borders exist.

I lived in the Yungas region from '92 to '94. There I came to see a process of drift with respect to the

old schemes of the Left, an extremely rapid reorganization of leftist ideas into Indianist discourse. From
there emerged the discourse of the native (*originario*),
which even in that moment I rejected, asking myself
who it was who wanted to see Indians in a museum
or in a cage like an endangered species.[11]

In these theoretical and practical comings and
goings, these biographical and collective twists
and turns, can be seen Silvia's forging of anticolonial theory from the South. It is important to
note that the first translation of the School of
Subaltern Studies of India was done in Bolivia, in
a collection edited by Silvia and Rossana Barragán.
In 1997 they published *Debates post coloniales.
Una introducción a los estudios de la subalternidad.*[12] This was a pioneering intervention and
a strategy for amplifying the arguments against
the neoliberal multiculturalism imposed by the
state as an official solution to internal colonialism.
That long horizon of debate and rebellion, which
encourages the opening of archives and research in
nonlinear time, allows Silvia to unsettle categories
and dethrone the texts consecrated by academic
fads. "The postcolonial is a desire, the anticolonial a struggle, and the decolonial an unpleasant
neologism," she says, as we chat in the streets of
Buenos Aires. This disobedience saved her from
making anticolonial theory into a question of guilt:
"We must deepen and radicalize difference: *in, with,*

and *against* the subaltern," she challenges. This is a formula that allows us also to escape the perverse relation constructed by the structure of "indigenous resentment, non-indigenous guilt," which functions, Silvia argues, as an affective basis for a populism wrapped in a discourse of the "native" as "ornamental."[13] It does not mean simply "inverting the hierarchy without touching the dualism (Guha *dixit*)" between colonizer and colonized and using the catchphrase of Eurocentrism to construct new limpid binaries. This declassificatory move that Silvia details is what permits her to understand even "'whitening' processes as survival strategies: we must distinguish those who gained power from those who wallowed in shame and those who are no longer pure." From this move, too, can come the power/strength of composite languages, along with the capacity to confront contingency and integrate outside forces. Indigeneity, from this perspective, cannot be an argument for purism.

Inventing a method: sociology of the image

Silvia Rivera Cusicanqui has taught for decades. She has taught for a long time at the Greater University of San Andrés (UMSA) in La Paz and in universities around the world. "Iconoclastic" and "irreverent" are two words she often says and that

reverberate in her classrooms like a mantra: first
you repeat them, later you taste them, and when
they acquire a rhythm and you intone them with
every breath, finally they open other pathways
of transmission. Thus we can translate them into
practical principles: to *wonder*, to *figure out*, and
to *communicate*.

With these three verbs, Rivera Cusicanqui synthesizes a series of *gestures*. First, the curiosity that
comes from a *peripheral gaze*: the gaze of the
vagabond, the gaze of the poetic figure of the *flâneur*
(again evoking Benjamin, one of her favorite philos-
ophers), that comes from the condition of passing
by, transiting, roaming, and thus has a capacity to
connect disparate elements. The peripheral gaze
incorporates a *bodily perception*. It concretizes
the idea of exploratory research and requires a
state of alertness. It is practiced in motion and
maintains a certain affinity with what has been
called creative attention. Figuring out, the second
step, is following a clue. It is the *focalized* gaze.
And for this step, Silvia insists, "the first step is
clarifying the *motivational 'why' that connects the
researcher and the research subject.*" She says this
to highlight an indispensable task: discovering "the
metaphorical connection between research topics
and lived experience,"[14] because only by scruti-
nizing this vital commitment to our "subjects" can
we venture true hypotheses, grounding our theory

so it appears in our writing as a wink rather than as rigid proof of authorization.

Finally, how to communicate? Talk *to* others, talk *with* others. There is an expressive-dialogic level that includes "modesty in inserting your voice" along with "a recognition of the authorial effects of listening," and finally the art of writing, or filming, or of finding collage-like formats. Speak after listening, because listening is also a mode of looking, a mechanism to create understanding as empathy, capable of becoming an element of intersubjectivity. Thus epistemology becomes an ethic, interviews a form of *happening*. And the key is respect for and management of the emotive energy of memory: its polyvalence beyond the lament and the epic, beyond the memorialism of the museum.

In this way, Silvia has constructed her own method, "sociology of the image," which is also the title of her 2015 book. The book contains methods that highlight her pedagogical experimentation, like *flashbacks,* and *déjà vu*, which she uses in her books but also in various videos she has scripted and filmed.[15] Through these multiple modes (and strongly influenced by Maurice Halbwachs and Ernst Bloch), Silvia understands collective memory as a series of montages that are updated according to the ebb and flow of struggle and are deployed as auspicious gestures of justice: "There is a guide we make for ourselves that has to do with the thoughts produced in moments of danger."

This is what allows her, for example, to forge an alliance with Felipe Guaman Poma de Ayala, the author of *First Chronicle of Good Government* (c.1612–1615), and read it according to her method. *First Chronicle* is a 1,000-page letter to the king of Spain with more than 300 ink drawings, which Silvia sheds light on through her "sociology of the image." This reading of the book allows us to smuggle Silvia herself into one of its drawings in an anachronistic superimposition. Montage (a method that already appears, for example, in *Los artesanos libertarios*) would give us a *poet-astrologer*: "walk, know, believe," verbs of thought in motion, with a horizon of an "intellectual craft" that does not allow the expropriation of the debate over what another idea of totality might look like. This is elaborated in *Principio Potosí Reverso*,[16] a catalogue-book Silvia made with El Colectivo 2, which narrates a history that moves from the colonial mines in one of the epicenters in our region to contemporary neoextractivism. The image, thus interrogated, becomes theory. Image is not illustration. It demands a trust in the autonomy of perception that consists of looking with the whole body. This formula is a whole program of counter-knowledge and counter-power: to look with the whole body is to grope with the skin, to listen with the back, to sound out with the feet, because again it is a series of *gestures* that decenter the gaze. To look with the whole body is to activate the visual sense of other organs: that is to say, to move toward a multilateral notion of the image, in which sight loses its predominance *just at the moment of seeing*. The question, Silvia clarifies, is "how we would decolonize Cartesian oculocentrism and reintegrate the body's gaze to the flow of inhabiting space-time, in what others call history."

It is clear that university is not always the site of theoretical invention. In Bolivia, the university was always an "elusive and distant" entity, in Silvia's words. This "disadvantage," however, became an advantage in the moment of connecting to books and to theory in general.

> We discovered European provincialism. For example, that the English don't read the French. Of course we can't see that from here because we attribute to them universality. But on this continent we are less provincial: we read everything that comes to us, under the selection principle that anything could serve us in a social emergency. Thus we have the luck of having skipped over various fads, because they arrived late or because they seem to come from another planet, and of having trained ourselves in an eclectic freedom.[17]

Having few books, in contrast with the "current hyperaccessibility," demanded of us that "we make use from our own vantage point of the texts we had, but also that we make fragile the certainty of our thought starting from reality, in line with the proposals of Marx, for whom the real was more important than thought."[18] Involve the whole body, put thought in a state of rebellion, and challenge the notion of scarcity.

Ch'ixi as a talisman-concept

For Silvia, epistemology is a decolonizing practice. She elaborates this practice through her concept of *ch'ixi*: a version of the notion of the "motley" conceptualized by the sociologist René Zavaleta Mercado,[19] with whom she maintained an intense political and intellectual exchange. "I believe it is a talisman-word, which allows us to speak beyond the emblematic identities of ethic politics. And I also believe it has its aura in certain states of collective availability that make words polysemic."

The word *ch'ixi* appears in the title of this volume, which was first published in 2010 by Retazos & Tinta Limón. The *ch'ixi* concept is the possibility of reconstructing the motley lexicon of *mestizaje* as a popular world strained by the requirements of decolonizing practices:

> I consider myself *ch'ixi* and consider it the most appropriate translation of the motley mix that we,

who are called *mestizas* and *mestizos*, are. The word *ch'ixi* has many connotations: it is a color that is the product of juxtaposition, in small points or spots, of opposed or contrasting colors: black and white, red and green, and so on. It is this heather gray that comes from the imperceptible mixing of black and white, which are confused by perception, without ever being completely mixed. The notion of *ch'ixi*, like many others (*allqa, ayni*), reflects the Aymara idea of something that is and is not at the same time. It is the logic of the included third. A *ch'ixi* color gray is white but is not white at the same time; it is both white and its opposite, black.[20]

Ch'ixi has the force of undifferentiation, and "[t]he potential of the undifferentiated is that it joins opposites."[21] As an image, it comes from the Aymara sculptor Victor Zapana, who explained to Silvia

which animals come from those rocks and why they are powerful animals. He then told me "*ch'ixinakax utxiwa*," which is to say emphatically: *ch'ixi* entities exist; they are powerful because they are indeterminate, neither white nor black but both at once. The snake is from above and at the same time from below; it is masculine and feminine; it does not belong to the sky nor the earth but inhabits both spaces, like rain or like an underground river, like lightning or like a seam in a mine.

Silvia proposes counterposing the notion of the *ch'ixi* (the motley) with that of *hybridity*, in an open polemic against Néstor García Canclini and the decolonial theorists who have used his work. The hybrid, she argues, expresses the idea that from the mix of two different entities emerges a third that is completely new: "a third race or social group with the capacity to merge the features of its ancestors in a harmonic and as yet unknown blend."[22] In this sense, the counterpoint provided by the notion of the motley is clear: there is no fusion of differences. There is antagonism and unresolved contradiction, and therefore difference sustains its "contentious" character.

Let us add one more point: this concept of the motley is deployed in another fundamental way. The "heteronymic pairs" of which Silvia speaks point us to ways of looking and talking that reveal the double face, ambivalence, contradiction, and reversal that always organizes things not into clear binaries, but rather into spaces with sliding boundaries and flickering edges, spaces where things exist and then cease to be, where they mutate, invert, or are contaminated by new relationships, uses, and meanings. This heteronymy evolves into a heterodoxy of thought and practice. And it reveals an analytical mode trained by ambiguity, by the cycles and transformations of things. This training allows Silvia to understand the "oblique and convoluted" paths and effects of Indian resistance.

The elaboration of *ch'ixi* practice moves us past the long debate about *mestizaje*. This connection leads us to another of Silvia's books, the essay collection *Violencias (re)encubiertas en Bolivia*,[23] which develops a "hypothesis about colonial Andean *mestizaje*," analyzing its ideological function as well as its variation and internal tension over different temporal horizons. She emphasizes that decolonization is a collective endeavor: "One cannot decolonize alone because, as Jim Morrison and also Foucault said, we carry the lords within us because of our cowardice and laziness."

This invective reveals another wrinkle in the critique of the "native" concept. Rivera Cusicanqui's criticism has focused especially on its use as official state rhetoric: "It is a word that divides us, that isolates Indians, and, above all, that negates their majority status and compels them to recognize themselves in a series of rights that confine them to official minority status from a state perspective." Additionally, important historical research has demonstrated the versatility of the figure of the native, as when Tristan Platt narrates the conversion of the outsider (*forastero*) into native. Identities are thus also effects of montage and – when they do not congeal in stereotypes – processes of becoming. "It must have to do with how in Bolivia instead of going to therapy, we go out partying," she speculates.

The irrevent *mestizo*, capable of shifting to a *ch'ixi* identity, draws on a current of women's alliance and feminist potency. Silvia writes,

> Where does my class traitorism come from? From the love I had for a woman named Rosa who took care of me when I was a child and died when I was eight years old. From then on I have been an eternal orphan, eternally nostalgic for this substitute mother. And I think this happened with many *mestizas* and *mestizos*, among others [La Paz-based feminist artist and activist] Maria Galindo, who wrote a beautiful piece that asks "must I have a *chola* among my ancestors?" which is obviously an homage to the *chola* who raised her. From this I have a whole hypothesis about the "*aguayo*[24] complex" that would come to be the root of modern populisms.[25]

The "*aguayo* complex" has become the formula for a fundamental problem: part of the affective foundations of racism.

> The *aguayo* complex occurs when you have loved this woman since babyhood, you have smelled her and believed her to be your mother, and then when you are seven years old your family teaches you to despise her. And the pain this produces in you is unforgivable. I have never forgiven my mother, even three years after her death, even with the rituals of all the saints. And for me to this day, Rosa's family is my real family. I have been to the cemetery to see Rosa more often than to see my mother. But Rosa's family has helped me when I try to forgive my mother. It is

very hurtful when you ask yourself as a child "why am I not allowed to love her?" It is something treated very well by the writer Rosario Castellanos; in her it is an incurable pain. For me it was recognizing the bilingualism of sounds I heard as a child. When I realized that what I speak is *castimillano*[26] and not Spanish, that I already know the dialect connector, the semiotic shifter, the translation key. The day I said, "finally, I can speak it?" and I spilled it all on the radio, overcoming even the shame that Aymaras would laugh at my bad Aymara, I realized that I was remembering back to four generations.[27]

The death of a discipline and the genesis of undiscipline

Silvia describes Aymara as an "agglutinative" language, because the same term can vary according to its suffix, context of enunciation, and with every operation of specific meaning, as well as according to rhetorical strategy. She subjects her own theory to this kind of variability as well, to the point of saying, "Some time ago I acquired the custom of publicly repudiating my previous work." It is not a minor point that this possibility is tied to a woman's trajectory: it redeploys the "advantage of disadvantage, the affirmative side of being devalued." It also irreverently performs the idea Silvia insists on of "our episteme," capable of including nonlinear and opposing terms, zones of conflict and encounter, new starting points. Working with failures (cognitive and political), with their sensitive information, is part of the process of reshaping thought, again and again, into a state of rebellion.

The passion in Silvia's voice, its precision and energy, comes from her *castimillano,* a neologism that mixes the words *castellano* (Spanish) and *imilla.* If *imilla* refers to an Aymara girl or adolescent at the *"waylacha"* age, the age when she becomes free and flirtatious, *castimillano* is a flirtatious and duplicitous form of Spanish, full of tactical double meanings.

This is why when Gayatri Spivak visited Bolivia, despite having a list of translators available, it was Silvia who took on the challenging task of simultaneous interpretation. Silvia was the one who could communicate the undiscipline of the text and of linear translation. "How does one translate into Spanish the term *double bind* as Spivak uses it? In Aymara there is an exact word for that and it doesn't exist in Spanish: *pä chuyma,* which means to have the soul divided by two impossible obligations." These translation exercises, for Silvia, reveal that in this day and age, all words are in question. "This is a sign of *Pachakutik,* of a time of change."

This is also a way to construct and assemble one's own voice, and through this process find it. The materials Silvia works with are part of this gambit: whether it be the cinema of Jorge Sanjinés or the watercolors of Melchor María Mercado – two precursors of sociology of the image, according to Silvia – they are read with an intrusive eye, at the same time with suspicion and unveiling their absences, highlighting their allegories, and insisting on their singularity. Sociology of the image, like almost three decades of oral history, is a strategy of intense combat that Silvia maintains against the limits of alphabetic writing to reconnect with the deep rivers of anticolonial vitality. Thus she links the necessity of the indigenous presence with the originality of its philosophy and not with the stereotype of native purity. As Silvia says in a session with Argentine prisoners:

> The irreplaceable voice is one's own. Telling your life story to a cellmate during a night of insomnia is co-investigating, being part of the craft of oral history. Thus the fundamental thing is to protect the freedom each person feels inside and to use it to read through affinity: you must feel that you master the reading, read only what smells best, from back to front, in pieces, and later, write as a gesture of care and of fidelity to yourselves, as an exercise of freedom.

She gave them a prescription, for her an unbeatable one: "When you write, breathe deeply. It is a craft, it is a gesture of a worker. And when you read what you've written, go back to breathing this way, until you feel like there is a rhythm. Texts need to learn to dance."

Again, we come to the question of *rhythm* that considers epistemology an artifact of the corporeal. Above we explained that looking with the whole body as another way of mistrusting ocularcentrism brings other organs into play, to the point of fine-tuning the gaze and lateralizing it toward that which stays hidden: "It is about knowing with the *chuyma*, which includes your lungs, heart, and liver. Knowing is breathing and beating. It involves a metabolism and a rhythm with the cosmos." Thus knowing is a bodily political practice that is repeated, that is composed but that also overflows: "The practice of the hunger strike and the days-long walk of the multitude had the value of silence and the generation of a collective rhythm and a collective breathing that became a true performance," she says, remembering the large marches in defense of the Isiboro Secure National Park and Indigenous Territory (TIPNIS) in 2011. "There are, in these spaces of the unsaid, a set of sounds, gestures, movements that carry the living traces of colonialism and that resist explicit articulation, because that articulation would cause discomfort and would challenge the comfortable dream of the liberal society."

The displacement of the centers is a fact, says Silvia. But in the peripheries, too, there is an impulse

to construct new centers. At the same time, and on
the contrary, there is a utopian dimension that
insists on displacement. That is what she argues in
her latest book, where the *ch'ixi* concept grows and
is expanded to a planetary scale, to propose that
"a *ch'ixi* world is possible."[28] This work develops
from an essay laying out a *ch'ixi* theory of value
all the way to the regime-toppling power of social
mobilizations, passing through "elemental" forms
of everyday resistance. It is a volume of interventions that were all first expressed orally and only
later passed into the stability of the written word.
This is another twist in Silvia's preoccupation with a
method where the stained tongue of orality projects
its particular influence onto modes of thought.

To close, I want to signal four operations of
theory that are practiced, like maneuvers, by Silvia
Rivera Cusicanqui. I believe they are lines of force
in her thought, gestures in her words, and practical
requirements. An inspiration for when thought
enters into a state of rebellion:

1 *An update of the anticolonial.* There are two
interventions into the ongoing discussion on our
continent that stand out in Silvia's anticolonial
method and in her way of narrating history. On the
one hand, the question of *development*: her work
illuminates the word's historical link to the doctrine
of *miserabilism* (under the sign of unproductiveness,

underdevelopment, and/or survival) as a descriptor of the popular and subaltern sectors, in the 1950s but also in the oligarchic representations of the nineteenth century, and continuing today under the sign of neodevelopmentalism. On the other hand, the emblematization of Indians and *cholos* (which again can be extended to the popular sectors in general) through their "ornamental subsumption" erases their profuse and diverse productive activity; their urban hegemony; their consciousness that is *ch'ixi*, motley, capable of heterogenous excess. These are both key interventions into too-often stagnant discussions in Latin America, interventions that put *the present* in tension with anticolonial critique from a place that is philosophical rather than purely ideological, academic, or moral.

2 A radical theory of difference from the perspective of the subaltern. In Latin America, the need in the 1990s to think about how minoritarian political rationalities seemed to be metabolized and pacified through neoliberal multiculturalism made evident the need to return to the evaluation of the condition of *domination.* An archive of the 1970s with Fanon readings in a regional key later linked with a translation (in the broad sense of the word) of the Subaltern Studies Group of India from the Southern Cone. This threatened the exclusive role of the US academy as translator of subaltern texts and mediator of subaltern knowledge. What remains clear (and what is fertile to think in terms of a theory of translation) are some *political conditions* of translation. We could summarize them thus: (1) the necessity of thinking political action beyond class and the Marxist canon; (2) the need to confront our immersion in power of the neoliberal multiculturalist variety; and finally (3) the necessity for theoretical exploration that does not have its privileged channel in the university – even though that problematizes its "dependent" character.

Of course the Gramscian Marxist thinkers in Latin America in the 1970s were pioneers in this type of "translation," and they, too, approached the also-Gramscian problem of "translatability": this current flowed from the Argentine José Aricó to the Bolivian René Zavaleta Mercado, from the Peruvian Alberto Flores Galindo to the Mexican Pablo González Casanova. Now those voices have become female ones. And Silvia Rivera Cusicanqui is one of the most audacious, because she has formulated the most radical critique of the decolonial lexicon now sacred in the academy, demonstrating the rebel sources of the erosion of national monolinguism.

3 An attempt at a theory of value, as seen from migrant routes. The becoming *ch'ixi* theory of value appears as a perspective that recovers the space of colonial migration. It is that which rebelled against colonial extraction, which persevered in the national modern territory and resisted neoliberalism because it was *capable of revisiting the long memory of the internal colonial market*: of the circulation over long distances of commodities, of the networks of productive – not salaried – communities and of the motley cultural centers. On this level, the motley urban centers were spaces of concretizing the projects of migrating to the city, nourished by the aspiration to "citizenship and urbanization" of successive generations "through access to cultural, symbolic, and material goods that," according to Silvia, "the society tenaciously kept from the Indian-peasant classes." This migrant trajectory, linked to the experience of the economic circuits, organizes the motley composition of the urban centers as well as their economies. It is on this level that the *ch'ixi* concept expresses its political and conceptual potency, giving this multicolored space the weight of a political, cultural, and economic current that is also completely contemporary, and has the power to restore our anticolonial vitality.

4 *The reclaiming of memory as insurgent practice.* How do you count a revolution? What counts as revolution? Under which historical horizon can we think insurgency and resistance but also sabotage of and jokes on the modalities of domination? These

questions press Silvia Rivera Cusicanqui to think in a layered way about historical time and the making of memory, that Benjaminian space of always-open contest. She thus animates an ambitious reconceptualization in historiographical terms and practical politics of other rationalities that show how the *colonial condition* structures political relationships and, in this way, stores up the scene of revolt as an ever-present possibility.

1

Another Bicentennial

The rebellion of Tupaq Katari in 1781 constituted part of a cycle of massive pan-Andean mobilizations that shook the entire region. These mobilizations occurred in reaction to Bourbon policies originating in the mid-eighteenth century which attempted to reinforce the crown's control over the colonial society and economy. These policies, which appeared in Spain as a set of progressive reforms in the commercial-capitalist sense, were imposed on the Andean colonies as a system of mercantilism. This system operated through the *reparto*, the forced distribution and sale of goods in indigenous communities. Peninsular magistrates used the *reparto* as a mechanism to coercively appropriate indigenous surplus and trade circuits, those new forms of indigenous commercial accumulation that had been developing since the sixteenth century in the space that was called *el trajín* (the hustle and bustle). In the eighteenth century, the market thus became the scene of colonial forms of coercion, which forced Indians to buy (and to go into debt buying) the *repartos*, which were legalized in 1750. The historiography of the pan-Andean uprisings has identified the *repartos* as the most visible structural cause of the collective discontent that culminated in the great rebellion of 1781, whose principal battle was the siege of the city of La Paz between March and October of that year, under the command of Julián Apaza-Tupaq Katari and his indigenous subcommanders.

If we look at the Katari rebellion from the vantage point of the present, we can see the memory of the actions projected forward in the cycle of uprisings and road blockades in 2000–2005, whose epicenter was the city of El Alto, also an insurgent headquarters in 1781. These recent events evoke an inversion of historical time, the insurgency of a past and a future, which might culminate in catastrophe or renewal. In 1781, the defeat of the Indians constructed lasting symbols of domination, through painting, theater, and oral traditions. In 2003–2005, that defeat was converted into victory for the insurgents. During these delirious moments of collective action, participants experience a change in consciousness, in identities and forms of knowing, and in modes of conceiving the political.

Accounts of the present, like the historiography of the eighteenth century, have underestimated and simplified the politics of indigenous communities, attributing them to the excesses and promises of a handful of *caudillos* (populist strongmen) and erasing the whole intense process of politicization of everyday life that occurs in these moments of rebellion. The historiography of the Tupaq Katari movement has frequently characterized the movement's radicalism and collective violence by starting from a series of essentialist attributions that refer to the "wild" and "irrational" character of Indians, and particularly of the "Aymara race."

The museums and historic sites of La Paz present equally contradictory interpretations of insurgent processes. The Costumbrist Museum of Riosiño Park, for example, exhibits Tupaq Katari as a quartered body. This scene had already been introduced in the theater: in 1786, just five years after the rebellion, the bloody episode was staged in La Paz in a pedagogical play directed at the masses.[1] The figures in the Costumbrist Museum follow in the popular tradition of the Alasitas market with plaster miniatures, but they show Katari in the moment of his quartering. The scene expresses the solitude of the indigenous body – separated from its community and tied to four horses – surrounded by executioners. But the image also carries distinct resonances for different audiences: some see a bloody Indian who got what he deserved, while others see a dismembered body that will reunify one day to inaugurate a new cycle of history.

In the Murillo House Museum on Jaen Street hangs a nineteenth-century painting by Florentino Olivares, a copy of a canvas lost at the end of the previous century. It depicts the Aymara blockade of a battle-ready city. A horde of thousands of dark bodies on the horizon confronts the marching cavalry and armed troops, but a few small details – the hanged victims of both sides – mark this as the memory of a dramatic struggle to the death. The urban terror was transformed into lynching; the city seems to persist in this ominous memory. Yesterday Indians swarming the heights, controlling the hills, dominating the landscape, and choking off the descent from el Alto and the Killi-Killi hillside; today rootless thieves and migrants transgressing the borders of society and threatening it with individualized violence.

The peak of Killi-Killi, where Katari's head was displayed after his quartering, has now become a tourist overlook that offers a splendid view of the La Paz basin. But every November 14 this "place of memory" summons *ayllus* and Aymara communities, Indianist political movements and ritual specialists, who call to continue the struggle and invoke the reunification of the fragmented political body of indigenous society.[2]

We have lived with these conflicting visions of history since the 1970s, when the CSUTCB reorganized under the aegis of the katarista movement, creating a massive road blockade in November 1979 that paralyzed communications and supplies in the cities for weeks. In this context, the threatening image of the horde returned, and residents of rich neighborhoods organized armed self-defense brigades to respond to the imminent violence of the insurgents. In 2003, the Indian siege expanded from El Alto to the residential zone of La Paz, where the communities of Apaña and Uni rose up. As in 1979, paranoia spread through the rich neighborhoods of Zona Sur. The state's reaction to this Indian siege was a typically colonial response to democratic demands for indigenous political participation: a preventive massacre. Both mobilizations drew sustenance from the 1781 process: the marches, blockades, the taking of hills, and the seizing of centers of power, as much as the repression and punitive violence against the insurgent multitude, have deep roots and form part of the collective memory of all the participants.

The most complete study of the Katari uprising cycle of 1781 is the doctoral thesis of Sinclair Thomson, the book version of which is called *We Alone Will Rule: Native Andean Politics in the Age of Insurgency*.[3] The author deliberately omits dates from the title in order to suggest resonances with the insurgency of the present. The book considers a long cycle of rebellions, identifying recurrent themes within them. These themes resurface in 1979 and in 2000–2005, reiterating the tactics and forms of symbolic struggle of the great rebellion, but also transforming them in the heat of the challenges and conditions of each historical moment. The themes return but the disjunctures and outcomes are different; the rebellion returns, but it is not the same. It is like a spiral movement. Historical memory is reactivated and at the same time reelaborated and resignified in subsequent crises and cycles of rebellion. It is evident that in a colonial situation, that which goes unsaid contains the most meaning; words mask more than they reveal, and symbols take center stage. It is through that brutal act of symbolic violence, the quartering of Katari, that Thomson organizes his research strategy, following the trail of Katari's body parts after his death in Peñas. The head was exhibited on the Killi-Killi hill on the eastern slope of La Paz. His right arm was carried to the Ayo Ayo plaza in Province Sicasica, his right leg to the Chulumani Plaza in the Yungas region, his left arm to the Achacachi Plaza in Omasuyos Province, and his left leg to the town of Caiquiaviri in Pacajes Province.[4] These four corners orient Thomson's search in the archives, and there he discovers links with the provinces of Chuccuito (in present-day Peru) and Larecaja (in the north of La Paz), defining a comprehensive territory of investigation while at the same time allowing for the deeper study of some cases and places that allows him to see long processes that unfold over decades.

The uprisings of the eighteenth century proposed a social order grounded in the recognition of differences, in the possibility of shared civility, and in legitimate authority. That new social order did not necessarily imply expulsion or extermination, but rather adopted the image of a restitution or reconstitution: the "world upside-down" (Felipe Guaman Poma de Ayala)[5] would restore the ethical foundations of the social order. A space of mediation would be constructed, thought and lived in its own syntax.

Here it is worth mentioning the depiction by this Quechua chronicler of two fundamental acts of the conquest: the capture and killing of the Inca emperor Atahualpa in 1532 and the execution of Tupaq Amaru I, the rebel Inca of Willkapampa. Through his drawings, Guaman Poma created a visual theory of the colonial system. To represent the death of Atahualpa, he drew the Inca emperor being decapitated with a big knife by Spanish functionaries. He repeated the same figure in the case of Tupaq Amaru I, executed in 1571. But only Amaru died by decapitation, while the Inca Atahualpa was killed by garrotte. The "error" of Guaman Poma reveals his own interpretation and theorization of these events: the death of the Inca was, effectively, a beheading of the colonized society. Undoubtedly there is here a notion of "head" that does not imply the usual hierarchy over the rest of the body: the head is the complement of the *chuyma* – emotions – and not their manager. Atahualpa's decapitation thus signals profound disorganization and disequilibrium in the political body of the indigenous society.

But this dismal premonitory vision, expressed in the 1781 cycle, can be contrasted with the image of the Astrologer and Poet Indian, the Indian who knows how to cultivate food, decipher the signs of time-space, and navigate the world beyond the contingencies of history.

CONQUEST
Atahualpa Inca was beheaded/Atahualpa died in the city of Cajamarca.[6]

GOOD GOVERNMENT
Topa Amaro beheaded in Cuzco.[7]

AN ASTROLOGER-POET who knows about the path of the sun, the moon, the eclipses, the stars, and the comets; of hours, days, months, and years; and about the four winds of the world, in order to sow crops, since ancient times.[8]

2

Sociology of the Image: A View from Colonial Andean History

I have argued for many years that a situation of internal colonialism persists in our countries. Below I will use this framework to discuss what I call "sociology of the image," considering how visual cultures, while helping to make sense of the social as they do in all societies, have here developed along their own path, at once revealing and updating many unconscious aspects of our particular social world. Our society is characterized by elements of the cultural and civilizational confrontation begun in 1532. Words have a peculiar function in colonialism: they conceal rather than designate, a function made particularly evident in the republican phase, during which the state adopted egalitarian ideologies while at the same time erasing the citizenship rights of the majority of the population. In this way, words became a fictional record, plagued with euphemisms that veiled reality instead of revealing it.

In this way, public discourse becomes a form of not saying. And these unsaid meanings and notions, these beliefs in racial hierarchy and in the inherent inequality of human beings, continue to incubate in our common sense, exploding once in a while in cathartic and irrational eruptions. We do not speak of racism, even though in recent times we have witnessed racist collective outbursts, in January 2007 in Cochabamba or in May 2008 in Sucre, which at first glance seem inexplicable. These outbursts reveal the hidden, buried forms of the cultural conflicts we cannot rationalize. We cannot even talk about them. We have trouble speaking, connecting our public language with our private one. We have trouble saying what we think and consciously noticing our unconscious conflicts and shames. These difficulties have shaped our rhetorical modes, creating speech conventions laden with double and unspoken meanings that orient our practices and divorce actions from public pronouncements.

Images offer us interpretations and social narratives which since precolonial times have illuminated the social landscape and offered us perspectives and critical understandings of reality. The transit between image and word is part of a method and pedagogical practice that, in a public university like the UMSA (Higher University of San Andrés, in La Paz), has allowed me to close the gaps between standard, learned Spanish and colloquial modes of speech, between the visual and lived experience of students – the majority migrants to the city, from Aymara or Quechua backgrounds – and their fumbling attempts to express their ideas in academic Spanish.

At the same time, from a historical perspective, images have allowed me to discover feelings that elude the censorship of official language. An example is the work of Felipe Guaman Poma de Ayala, whose work was unknown for centuries but has now become the subject of multiple academic studies. His *First New Chronicle and Good Government* is a 1,000-page letter, written between 1612 and 1615 and addressed to the king of Spain, featuring more than 300 ink drawings. The language in which Guaman Poma writes abounds with terms from spoken Quechua, turns of phrase from Aymara songs and *jayllis* (songs of triumph), and notions like the "world upside-down," derived from the cataclysmic experience of conquest and colonization.

The world upside-down is a recurring idea in Guaman Poma, and it forms part of what I consider his visual theorization of the colonial system. More than in the written text of the chronicle, it is in the drawings that his own ideas unfold about pre-Hispanic indigenous society, about its values and its concepts of time-space, and about the meanings of the bloodbath that was the colonization and subordination of the population and territory of the Andes to the Spanish crown.[1]

The first important idea in Guaman Poma's work is that of order/disorder. Various sequences of his drawings address this theme. At the beginning of his chronicle, he shows different types of orders or groupings: the order of ages; the order of "paths" and spatial distribution in population centers; and the ritual calendar. Despite having adopted the Gregorian calendar, the sequence shows us another order, that of the relations between humans and the sacred world, which accompanies productive labor as much as communal coexistence and state rituals. But instead of detailing the injuries of the conquest, the abuses of the magistrate, and the brutal usurpations and injuries perpetrated out of ambition for gold and silver, Guaman Poma returns to the calendar, this time stripped of pagan ritual. Through this contrast, he shows us a productive order that is not exempt from ritual and devotion, in which months and labors go by and in which the Catholic saints' day calendar is linked with work routines. This order is grounded in the earth and has clear links with the ritual calendar of the first pages. In this way, the sequence puts into evidence the centrality of food and productive labor to the indigenous cosmic order. In the chronicle, this is a convincing argument against the usurpation of land and the exploitation of labor. To convince the king to install order and good government in his colonies, Guaman Poma exclaims: "With food God and his majesty is served, and with food we worship God. Without food there is neither man nor strength."[2] The presentation of the agricultural calendar thus has a pedagogical aim: "You must consider the poor Indians of this kingdom, seeing all these months how much you eat at the cost of the poor Indians of this kingdom of Peru."[3] This is a satisfactory ending to a long catalog of deprivation, pointing out that the foundations of every society and every government lie in the productive labor of agricultural workers.

The ritual calendar described at the beginning of the chronicle can now be seen from another perspective: its base sustains an equilibrium between the earth and the cosmic order represented by the stars, the mountains, and the elements. Despite Guaman Poma's adoption of the Gregorian calendar, which starts in January and ends in December, this entire cycle establishes a state ritualism and an order of good government. This sense of the common good is based in multiple relations: of humans with nature, of families with community, of communities with their authorities and with their Inca. The group of relations obeys a cosmic order, in which the rulers, the ruled, and the earth that nourishes them all converse. In contrast with the conquistadors' dogged obsession with precious metals, which Guaman Poma will depict in subsequent chapters, here he emphasizes the variety of sacrificial objects and the precision of their relationships with the space they inhabit or the particular moment of the offering.

Guaman Poma's description of spatial order also has an enlightening ending, which is structured by the contrast between pre- and post-conquest life. The drawings communicate social hierarchies through the organization of space, distinguishing the ages and sexes of the figures depicted in a structure from greater to lesser prestige and recognition. These hierarchies are expressed in "paths" occupied by distinct strata of men and women, who function as a mirror of the social hierarchy. We see the ordering of the women's space. In the "first path," the most esteemed site, we find weaving women between 33 and 50 years old.

The second "path" is occupied by women between 50 and 80 years old, the third by women older than 80, and the fourth by the disabled and infirm women who, as we saw in the month of August, performed ritual functions that meant they were located higher in the hierarchy than young marriageable women. The fifth path is thus the place for single women younger than 33. Here there is an esteem for work and experience which contrasts radically with the cult of youth and beauty which characterized the invading society. However, the text does show a series of pejorative conceptions of older women: 50-year-olds "are called old woman, widow, fallen woman. No attention was paid to such women." However, these women "were respected as honorable old women, and they had the maidens in their charge, and they assisted in other *mitas* (obligations) of their pueblos."[4] The esteem for these women's work contrasts with both their greed and the loss of prestige they experience under the colonial system. About women of 80 years, Guaman Poma says that previously "old women and orphans who were unable [to work the land] had no need of begging for alms; rather, these old women would feed and raise the orphaned children."[5] While now:

> There is no one to do the same for boys and girls, even when the old women can work. Because they refuse to bend their backs, the old women become poor; while poor, they have fantasies of becoming masters. But even though she is not the master, the commoner woman still makes herself into a noble-woman, and there you have the world upside-down.[6]

By outlining these social orders, Guaman Poma shows the temporal and spatial organization of indigenous society, understood as a just order and "good government." His argumentative and critical intention becomes visible when we compare some drawings with others in order to explore the parallels and contrasts, the reiteration of composition styles, and the organization of the series. In a certain way, this exercise has already been done by Rolena Adorno, who analyzed the internal dividing lines of the drawings, highlighting the symbolic values of the right and left, the upper and lower, the use of diagonals and the central spaces, to argue that hidden there was a type of Andean unconscious and an indigenous conception of space. However, this now-common structuralist or semiotic approach to Guaman Poma's work, like the idea of his indigenous alterity, leaves me unsatisfied. In a rather arbitrary manner, I instead apply to these drawings anachronistic notions, taken from cinema studies, such as sequence or flashback, in order to explore other hypothetical avenues of his thought. Either in contraposition or as a complement to his written language, these ideas seem to point to his comprehension, critique, and above all desire to communicate what he saw as the most important features of the colonial system. Using these alternative methods, I find that the conceptual and theoretical elements in his drawings can be transformed into powerful critical arguments. These arguments, which we might call Guaman Poma's iconographic theory of the colonial situation, indicate that legitimate domination and good government were impossible in the colonial context, a conclusion that can easily be extended to present-day Andean republics.

If we return to the image of the pre-Hispanic weaver, we can see that its eloquent commentary begins to thematize the relationship between labor exploitation and moral disorder. Between weaving as a sign of maturity and prestige, and weaving as a sign of coercion at the hands of doctrinaire priests, lies an abyss, but the text's meaning is lost if we only contemplate the two final images. The colonization of the realm of labor is comparable to the modern sweatshop. A conception of work as punishment pervades Western thought, from the Bible to Marxist thinkers like Enrique Dussel. But if we "flash back," if we recover the notion of coexistence between nature and human beings expressed in the order of the paths and calendric rituals, even despite its hierarchies and patriarchal traditions, we access a more severe and profound critique of labor exploitation, one which frames it as a moral outrage and an attack on human dignity rather than just the extraction of surplus value.

A second example of these insights occurs in a scene of magistrates, in which the magistrate's relatives and servants, seated at his table, eat and drink lavishly, while the character in close-up collects the leftovers in a bag. The person is an adult Indian, not a child, which is clear even though the bodies of those seated at the table are out of proportion. We can see here an indigenous conceptualization of the notion of oppression. In Aymara and Quechua, words for "oppression" and "exploitation" do not exist. Both ideas are summarized in the Aymara notion of *"jisk'achasina"* of *"jisk'achaña"*: belittling, which is associated with the humble condition of servitude.

Humiliation and disorder go hand in hand: the world upside-down reverses hierarchies, putting servants in the condition of masters, carving out illegitimate paths for social ascension. In the text, Guaman Poma speaks of natural hierarchies, of preserving the distance between the high and the low, the superior and the inferior. He seems to have internalized the Spaniards' racial discourse, but at the same time he reveals the existence of a pre-Hispanic hierarchical order, which he represents as more legitimate. Nevertheless, the image of an Indian diminished in front of his equals maps a psychological itinerary of domination. The condition of social diminishing, the attitude of "bending one's back" or "lowering oneself," summarizes the moral background for colonial misery. More than physical pain, it is the dispossession of dignity and the internalization of the values of the oppressors that, as in the case of Frantz Fanon, make Guaman Poma into a theorist of the colonial condition.

Another contribution Guaman Poma makes to understanding the colonial foundations of society is his discovery that the relations colonialism inaugurates are founded on an original image: the nonhuman condition of the other. This ignorance and negation, as Jan Szeminski has shown, was not the sole property of the Spanish gaze; the Indians, too, came to deny the humanity of the recently arrived Spaniards.[7] This vision of Spanish radical otherness to indigenous eyes is expressed in another drawing, which belongs in the series on the conquest. According to Guaman Poma, when the advance-guard conquistador Pedro de Candia interviewed the Inca Wayna Qapaq, they held this dialogue:[8]

Wayna Qapaq: *Cay coritachu micunqui?* (You eat this gold?)

Candia: We eat this gold.[9]

What follows is a game of stereotypes and fantastical representations: in Spain, this encounter will reveal the existence of an empire of legend, in which the carpets, the clothes, the flags, and the utensils are pure gold. Years later, with Inca Wayna Qapaq dead and the kingdom wrapped up in a war of succession between Atahualpa and his brother Huáscar, the conquistadors, with Pizarro and Almagro at the head, prepared an ambush of Inca Atahualpa. But Atahualpa had been told about the Spaniards, and Guaman Poma emphasizes the doubt and the horror that suffused the tales of the foreigners:

> Atahualpa Inca was informed, as were the noble lords, captains, and the other Indians, about the lives of the Spaniards. What they heard frightened them: the Spaniards never slept – they said this because the Spaniards set watches. They ate silver and gold, both the Spaniards and their horses. They wore silver *ojotas* (sandals) – they said this because of the horse-shoes and bridles, and because of their steel weapons and red caps. And that day and night they spoke each with his papers, *quilca*. They all wore funeral shrouds. Their whole faces were covered in wool, and only their eyes could be seen. [...] They had very long pricks, which they wore dangling behind them – they said this because of their swords. They were all dressed in pure silver. And finally, they had no senior lord, because they all seemed like brothers in their clothes, speech, conversation, eating, and dressing, and they all had the same face; but it seemed to [the Indians] that they had one old gentleman with a dark face and white teeth and eyes, and that only this man spoke a lot to all of the others.[10]

Imagined as gold- and silver-eaters with enormous sexual attributes, shrouded like cadavers by their beards as they speak at night with their papers, the Christian Spaniards' corporeality pushes the boundaries of the human. But their forms of relating to one another are no less incomprehensible: the one who commands the others has no symbol to distinguish himself, except speaking "a lot to all of the others," the opposite of the silent and symbolic command of the Inca. Strangeness, stupor, and the idea that a cosmic cataclysm must be at the heart of their impotence loomed over the thousands of Inca soldiers, who could not conquer an army of barely one hundred sixty men, with arms and animals they had never seen before. In a previous moment, the siege of Cuzco by the rebel Incas, under the command of Manco Inca, introduces new shades into the acculturated discourse of Guaman Poma. According to the written text, the intervention of the Virgin Mary and that of the powerful Santiago Indiankiller, who was immediately associated with the terrible Illapa, god of lightning, would have given the victory to the besieged Spaniards. But in the drawing, ideas flow in a more subtle way. While Guaman Poma has chosen to represent the Spaniard and the Inca in a symmetrical position, with Candia on his knees and the Inca seated in a seemingly amicable and horizontal conversation, the text of the dialogue introduces a disjuncture and a contradiction. Gold as food dispossesses the visitor of his human condition, and synthesizes the astonishment of the indigenous society and the ontological distance between them and their invaders. This is a central metaphor of the conquest and of colonization. Its vigor allows us to leap from the sixteenth century to the present, from historiography to politics, to denounce and combat food transformed into gold, seeds turned into nuggets of death, and the ruin of humanity as a wound to nature and to the cosmos.

Historicist readings, appreciations based on the idea of authenticity and authorship, have done even more damage to Guaman Poma's work. An enormous quantity of studies have set out to show the falsehoods and inventions of this chronicler, his use of other texts, and the imprecision of much of his information and characters. The case of Candia is eloquent: he never in reality interviewed Wayna Qapaq, and it was not him but rather Pizarro who traveled to Spain with the gold of the Inca. The rigid vision of the academic critic has thus overlooked the interpretive value of the image, sticking to a notion of "historical truth" rather than the conceptual and moral framework of the person who writes or draws.

The same thing occurs with the representation of the two famous executions I referred to above: the death of Atahualpa in 1533 and that of Tupaq Amaru I in 1570. The drawings of both episodes are almost identical (see images on pages 9–10): the legitimate Inca and the rebel Inca of Willkapampa laid out, each man's body oriented in the same way while a Spaniard severs his head with a big knife and another man holds him by his feet. We now know that Atahualpa did not die in this way, but rather was subjected to the punishment of the garrotte. In the case of Tupaq Amaru I, the representation is more faithful, and the experiential proximity to the chronicler is more evident. But projecting this vision of the conquest and the death of Atahualpa was not justified by a lack of sources. Could it possibly be that Guaman Poma's account was grounded in false versions; that he fell victim to disinformation or ignorance? Since we are dealing with such important historical characters, does not this "error" merit something more than a correction or a historiographical clarification?

The similarity of the figures induces a flashback effect, allowing us to see them as an interpretation rather than a description of events. Indigenous society was decapitated. This image was rooted in the myths of the Inca Ri (whose head grew under the ground, until one day it was reunited with his body), which even now are recounted in communities in southern Peru. It is thus a moral and political perception of what happened: the deprivation of the head, as much as taking the roof off a house, or cutting one's hair, was considered in Andean society a maximum offense, the result of an essential enmity. It is precisely this radical destructiveness that serves as a metaphor for the social facts of conquest and colonization. The irony of "good government" accentuates Guaman Poma's argumentative intention and is revealed in the judgments that pour out in his writing: "How can the king, a prince, a duke, a count, a marquis, or even a gentleman be sentenced to death by his own servant, a poor gentleman? The only name for this is rising up and yearning to be higher than the king."[11]

But, in contrast with Atahualpa, who died alone, surrounded by Spaniards, Tupaq Amaru I was mourned by Indians, and it is their exclamations in Quechua that made explicit this unceasing enmity. ("*Ynga Wana Cauri, maytam rinqui? Spara aucaunchiccho mana huchayocta concayquita cuchon*" Inca Wana Cauri, where have you gone? Our perverse enemy will cut your neck, though you are innocent.[12]) Ethical judgment and historical interpretation signal here the contours of a look to the past, capable of "lighting the spark" of future rebellions, since "not even the dead will be safe from the enemy if he is victorious."[13]

This dismal and premonitory vision, expressed historically in the great rebellion of 1781 (Tupaq Amaru II, Tupaq Katari, and other emblematic figures of that interrupted continuity), can still be contrasted with the image of the Astrologer and Poet Indian (see p. 11), he who knows how to cultivate food, beyond the contingencies of history.

This figure is a poet, in the Aristotelean sense of the term: creator of the world, producer of food, expert in the cycles of the cosmos. And this poiesis of the world, realized on the journey through it, by the *kipus* (knotted cords) that register memory and the regularities of astral cycles, points us to a proposal: to see indigenous otherness as a new universality that opposes chaos and the destruction of the world and life. From ancient times through the present, it has been the weavers and astrologer-poets of the communities and villages who have revealed to us this alternative and subversive thread of knowledges and practices capable of restoring the world and setting it on its rightful course.

JANUARY

In January (Qapaq Raimi Killa, Festival of the Lords), we offer our own bodies, with fasting and pilgrimages to sacred places.[14]

FEBRUARY

In February (Paucar Warai Killa, month to dress in precious clothing), the kingdom "sacrificed a great sum of gold and silver and livestock at the specified sacred sites: sun, moon, star, and *waca willka*, on the highest hills and snow-capped mountains."[15] Additionally, the drawing shows guinea pigs and mollusk shells, as accompaniments to the precious metals.

MARCH

In March (Pacha Puquy, month of the maturation of the earth) comes the time to express thanks for the first fruits with the sacrifice of black llamas.[16]

ABRIL
CAMAI·IИCAPAIMİ

fiesta del ynga

APRIL
April is the time of rejoicing and state ritual. *Camai, Inka Raimi* (rest, celebrate the Inca): songs to the llamas and the rivers, public banquets and games, guests from all around the empire congregate in Cuzco.[17]

MAY

May (Jatuin Kusqui, month of the harvest) emphasizes the centrality of food to the ritual calendar: the search refers to the *illas*, rocks that represent the generative power of the earth and its fertility. The drawing reiterates the abundance and coordinated movement of the transport of the harvest to the community or estate storehouses.[18]

JUNE

June (Jawkay Kuski) is the little festival of the Inca: the season in which the authorities must visit "the officials and the Indians of this kingdom, so that the kingdom creates abundant food, so that everyone is sustained, so the poor like the rich can eat."[19]

JULY

In July the lands are distributed (Chacra Conacuy), with great offerings and sacrifices, Waylla Wiza, the ritual specialist, resembles the contemporary *yatiris* who burn offerings starting at the end of June.[20]

AGOSTO
CHACRAIAPVI
quilla

tiempo de labransa — haillinmi ynca —

AUGUST

August (month of breaking up the earth, Chacra
Yapuy Killa). The image represents the ritual sowing,
and the hunchbacked dwarf woman reveals the ritual
importance of bodily defects for summoning fertility
and ordering the chaotic world of the Manquapacha.
It was a month of general ritual in all communities,
with song, food, and drink accompanying the festive
moment of the planting.[21]

SEPTEMBER
September, Coia Raimi, festival of the queen, festival of the planets and stars, because the Coya (daughter of the Inca) is the queen of the sky. But it is also the month of illness and pestilence, which can be combated through ritual means.[22]

OCTOBER
October is the ritual of calling the rain. Uma Raimi
Killa. A black ram helps to cry and to ask for water
from god with his hunger; a sacrifice of white and
black llamas helps them cry from hunger and thirst to
call the rain.[23]

NOVEMBER

November, month of the dead. Aya Markai Killa. This time the offering is made to deceased ancestors, who emerge from their graves and join in the festivals and banquets of the living.[24]

DECEMBER
The cycle closes with a great festival of the sun
(Qapaq Raimi) of December, perhaps the moment of
the greatest concentration of symbolic state power, in
which quantities of gold, silver, and animal and human
sacrifices are buried.[25]

PRIMERA CALLE
AVACOCVARMI

se eran de treyta y tres años

FIRST PATH. AWACOC WARMI
"They were 33 years old and they married; before that, they were virgins and maidens."[26]

PADRES: FORCING THE INDIAN WOMEN
TO WEAVE CLOTH BY ACCUSING THEM OF
HAVING LOVERS – they beat them and do not pay.
In the *doctrina* (parish). "The *doctrina* padres compel
widows and single women to spin and weave, accusing
them of having lovers as an excuse for making them
work without paying them. In this way, Indian women
become whores and there is no remedy."[27]

PRIESTS: THE DOMINICAN FRIAR IS FURIOUS AND ARROGANT

They imprison single women and widows, accusing them of being concubines. They imprison them in their houses and force them to spin, weave *cunbe* (finely woven) clothing, and this is common throughout the kingdom, in the *doctrinas*. "Those friars are so bad-tempered and arrogant, with so little fear of God or justice, that in the *doctrina* they would punish cruelly and mete out justice. All they do is force single and widowed women to spin and weave clothing. And thus from so much pain the Indians were separated from their people."[28]

THE *CORREGIDOR* INVITES THE TOWN TO A
MEAL
At his table, lowly people, Indians working *mita* shifts,
mestizos, mulattoes, tributary Indians/*Corregidor*:
"a toast, señor Curaca"/tributary Indian: "Lord, our
Lord, *noca ciruiscayqui*" (Lord, my lord, I will serve
you)/Provinces.[29]

CONQUEST. GUAINA CAPAC INCA CANDIA,
ESPAÑOL
Cay coritachu micunqui (You eat this gold?)/We eat
this gold/in Cuzco.[30]

3
Ch'ixinakax utxiwa:
A Reflection on the Practices and Discourses of Decolonization

The colonial condition obscures a number of paradoxes. Throughout Andean history, the modernizing efforts of the Europeanized elites in the region resulted in successive waves of recolonization. One example is the Bourbon reforms that both preceded and followed the great cycle of rebellion from 1771 to 1781. Although it is true that modern history meant slavery for the indigenous peoples of America, it was simultaneously an arena of resistance and conflict, a site for the development of sweeping counterhegemonic strategies, and a space for the creation of new indigenous languages and projects of modernity.[1] The condition of possibility for an indigenous hegemony is located in the territory of the modern nation – inserted into the contemporary world – and is once again able to take up the long memory of the internal colonial market, of the long-distance circulation of goods, of networks of productive communities (waged or unwaged), and of the multicultural and multicolored [*abigarrados*] urban centers. In Potosí, the large market of coca and silver was called El Gato ("the cat," a Castilianization of the indigenous *qhatu*), and the *qhateras* (merchants) were emblematic of indigenous modernity. They were the last link in the production and sale of these goods that were fully modern and yet grounded in indigenous technologies and knowledges.[2] The bustling colonial space was also the site that linked indigenous leaders of Tupaq Amaru II, Tupaq Katari, and Tomás Katari to long-distance mercantile circulation.[3] And it was the experience of the Spanish crown's commercial levying – not only the royal fifth, the checkpoints, and tithes or other tax burdens, but also the monopoly on coca, the forced distribution of goods, and the coercive recruitment of porters and shepherds [*llameras*] – that unleashed the fury of rebellion. Against the financial and predatory forms of coercive taxation, the Katari–Amaru project was the expression of indigenous modernity in which religious and political self-determination signified a retaking of their own historicity – a decolonization of imaginaries and of the forms of representation. Such actions demonstrate that we indigenous were and are, above all, contemporary beings and peers, and in this dimension [*aka pacha*], we perform and display our own commitment to modernity. Cultural postmodernism, imposed by the elites and reproduced by the state in a fragmented and subordinate way, is alien to us as a tactic.[4] There is no *post* or *pre* in this vision of history that is not linear or teleological but rather moves in cycles and spirals and sets out on a course without neglecting to return to the same point. The indigenous world does not conceive of history as linear; the past–future is contained in the present. The regression or progression, the repetition or overcoming of the past is at play in each conjuncture and is dependent more on our acts than on our words. The project of indigenous modernity can emerge from the present in a spiral whose movement is a continuous feedback from the past to the future – a "principle of hope" or "anticipatory consciousness" – that both discerns and realizes decolonization at the same time.[5]

The contemporary experience commits us to the present – *aka pacha* – which in turn contains within it the seeds of the future that emerge from the depths of the past [*qhip nayr uñtasis sarnaqapxañani*]. The present is the setting for simultaneously modernizing and archaic impulses, of strategies to preserve the status quo and of others that signify revolt and renewal of the world: *Pachakuti*. The upside-down world created by colonialism will return to its feet as history only if it can defeat those who are determined to preserve the past, with its burden of ill-gotten privileges. But if the preservers of the past succeed, the past cannot escape the fury of the enemy, to paraphrase Walter Benjamin.[6]

Who really are the archaic and conservative groups and classes in Bolivia? What is decolonization, and what does it have to do with modernity? How can the exclusive, ethnocentric "we" be articulated with the inclusive "we" – a homeland for everyone – that envisions decolonization? How have we thought and problematized, in the here and now, the colonized present and its overturning?

In 1983, when Aníbal Quijano still spoke of the movements and uprisings of the Andean peasantry as "pre-political" (in a text that I fittingly criticized[7]), I was writing *Oppressed but Not Defeated*, which provided a radically different reading of the significance and relevance of the indigenous protests in the Andes to the struggles of the present. In this text, I argued that the Katarista–Indianista uprising of 1979 made clear for Bolivia the necessity of a "radical and profound decolonization" in its political, economic, and, above all, mental structures – that is, the country's ways of conceiving the world.[8]

The book's conclusion resulted from a detailed analysis of different historical moments of domination in our country: the colonial, liberal, and populist horizons that not only reversed the legal and constitutional orderings but also recycled old practices of exclusion and discrimination. Since the nineteenth century, liberal and modernizing reforms in Bolivia have given rise to a practice of conditional inclusion, a "mitigated and second class" citizenship.[9] But the price of this false inclusion has been the archaism of the elites. Recolonization made the reproduction of feudal and rentier modes of domination possible, modes based on the privileged ascriptions granted by the colonial center of power. Today, the rhetoric of equality and citizenship is converted into a caricature that includes not only tacit political and cultural privileges but also notions of common sense that make incongruities tolerable and allow for the reproduction of the colonial structures of oppression.

Bolivian elites are a caricature of the West. In speaking of them, I refer not only to the political class and the state bureaucracy but also to the intelligentsia that strikes postmodern and even postcolonial poses, and to the US academy and its followers who built pyramidal structures of power and symbolic capital – baseless pyramids that vertically bind certain Latin American universities – and form clientelist networks with indigenous and black intellectuals.

The cultural studies departments of many North American universities have adopted "postcolonial studies" in their curricula with an academicist and culturalist stamp devoid of the sense of political urgency that characterized the intellectual endeavors of their colleagues in India. Although the majority of the founders of the journal *Subaltern Studies* formed part of the Bengali elite in the 1970s and 1980s – many of them graduated from the University of Calcutta – their difference was located both in language, in the radical alterity that it represented to speak Bengali, Hindi, and other languages in India, and in a long tradition of written culture and philosophical reflection. Yet, without altering anything of the relations of force in the "palaces" of empire, the cultural studies departments of North American universities have adopted the ideas of subaltern studies and launched debates in Latin America, thus creating a jargon, a conceptual apparatus, and forms of reference and counterreference that have isolated academic treatises from any obligation to or dialogue with insurgent social forces. Walter Mignolo and company have built a small empire within an empire, strategically appropriating the contributions of the subaltern studies school of India and the various Latin American variants of critical reflection on colonization and decolonization.

Domestically, the Bolivian elites have adopted an official multiculturalism that is riddled with references to Will Kymlicka and anchored in the idea of indigenous people as minorities. Across Latin America, massive protests were triggered against neoliberal policies in Venezuela (1989), Mexico (1994), Bolivia (2000–2005), and Argentina (2002) that alerted the technocrats of the necessity to "humanize" structural adjustment. The immediate consequence of this was an ornamental and symbolic multiculturalism with prescriptions such as "ethno-tourism" and "eco-tourism," which draw on a theatricalization of the "originary" condition of a people rooted in the past and unable to make their own destiny.

In 1994, in an effort to hide the business of "capitalization," Bolivian president Gonzalo Sánchez de Lozada adopted the culturist agenda of indigeneity, through his symbolic vice president (Víctor Hugo Cárdenas), municipal decentralization, and constitutional reform. Whether it was for fear of the rabble or to follow the agenda of their financiers, the elites were sensitive to the demands for recognition and political participation of indigenous social movements and adopted a rhetorical and essentialist discourse centered on the notion of "original people." This recognition – truncated, conditional, and reluctant – of indigenous cultural and territorial rights allowed for the recycling of the elites and the continuation of their monopoly on power. What did this reappropriation mean, and what were its consequences? The Kataristas and Indianistas, based in the western Andes, had a schematic view of the eastern peoples and spoke of "Aymaras," "Qhichwas," and "Tupiguaranís," or simply of "Indians." Simultaneously, the notion of origin refers us to a past imagined as quiet, static, and archaic, which allows us to see the strategic recuperation of indigenous demands and the neutralization of the decolonizing impulse. A discussion of these communities situated in the "origin" denies the contemporaneity of these populations and excludes them from the struggles of modernity. They are given a residual status that, in fact, converts them into minorities, ensnaring them in indigenist stereotypes of the noble savage and as guardians of nature.

And so, as the indigenous people of the east and west are imprisoned in their *tierras communitarias de origen* (original communal lands) and are NGOized, essentialist and Orientalist notions become hegemonic, and the indigenous people are turned into multicultural adornment for neoliberalism.[10] The new stereotype of the indigenous combines the idea of a continuous territorial occupation, invariably rural, with a range of ethnic and cultural traits, and classifies indigenous behavior and constructs scenarios for an almost theatrical display of alterity. Rossana Barragán calls this strategy of cholo-indigenous ethnic self-affirmation an "emblematic identity."[11]

But the multicultural discourse also conceals a secret agenda to deny the ethnicity of the multi-colored [*abigarradas*] and acculturated populations – the settlement areas, mining centers, indigenous commercial networks in the internal and black markets, the cities. This agenda allowed the elites and the technobureaucracy of the state and the NGOs to comply with the dictates of empire: "*zero coca*" forced eradication and closure of legal markets in the tropics of Cochabamba, intellectual property laws, tax reform, and the liquidation of contraband.[12] The term "original people" affirms and recognizes but at the same time obscures and excludes the large majority of the Aymara- and Qhichwa-speaking population of the subtropics, the mining centers, the cities, and the indigenous commercial networks of the internal and black markets. It is therefore a suitable term for the strategy of depriving indigenous peoples of their potentially hegemonic status and their capacity to affect the state.[13]

The official multiculturalism described above has been the concealing mechanism par excellence for new forms of colonization. The elites adopt a strategy of crossdressing and articulate new forms of cooptation and neutralization. In this way, they reproduce a "conditional inclusion," a mitigated and second-class citizenship that molds subaltern imaginaries and identities into the role of ornaments through which the anonymous masses play out the theatricality of their own identity.

What, then, is decolonization? Can it be understood as only a thought or a discourse? I think that this question is another central point that has been barely alluded to in contemporary debates. Modernizing discourse, such as that of the liberals at the end of the nineteenth century, could have existed only if it had been accompanied by liberal practices, by genuine operations of equality and coparticipation in the public sphere. By recognizing what was only an ill-intentioned and rhetorical equality for the Indians, the Ley de Exvinculación of October 5, 1874, canceled the liberal reforms and formalized, after the fact, an aggressive recolonization of indigenous territories throughout the country, resulting in a massive expansion of large estates through the expropriation of communal lands. Meanwhile, the elites were engaged in rent-seeking activities, long trips to Europe, and, above all, speculative investment in land and mining concessions. The "illustrious" people at the time, such as the "scientists" of the Mexican Porfiriato [the much-hated rule of Mexican president Porfirio Diaz 1876–1911], constructed, with strong support of the state apparatus (the army, in particular), a rentier and aristocratic class that was not only more colonial than that of the Spanish aristocracy but also more archaic and precapitalist. In effect, the nineteenth-century oligarchy remained aloof from the commercial and industrial activities that characterized their sixteenth-century ancestors and was instead dedicated to the usurpation of land, speculation, and import–export trade. The exploitation of materials, primarily under the control of foreign capital and long-distance internal markets (which includes very large cross-border spaces in all the neighboring countries), fell into the hands of indigenous and *mestizo* populations with large urban–rural networks and links to the expanded reproduction of capital. It was, therefore, the practice of the diverse productive collectives – including those who "produced" circulation – that defined the modern condition, while the modernizing discourse of the elites only served to mask their archaic processes of cultural and political conservatism, which reproduces and renews the colonial condition throughout society.

There can be no discourse of decolonization, no theory of decolonization, without a decolonizing practice. The discourse of multiculturalism and the discourse of hybridity are essentialist and historicist interpretations of the indigenous question. They do not address the fundamental issues of decolonization but instead obscure and renew the effective practices of colonization and subalternization. Their function is to supplant the indigenous populations as historical subjects and to turn their struggles and demands into elements of a cultural reengineering and a state apparatus in order to subjugate them and neutralize their will. A "change so that everything remains the same" bestows rhetorical recognition and subordinates, through patronage, the Indians into purely emblematic and symbolic functions – that is, a sort of "cultural *pongueaje*" [a free domestic service required of indigenous tenants] in the service of the spectacle of the multicultural state and mass communication.

The *gatopardismo* [the policy of changing everything so that everything remains the same] of the political and economic elites is reproduced in miniature in the social sciences that study the Andean region. Here we find a typical structure of "internal colonialism" as defined by Pablo González Casanovas in 1969.[14] The arboreal structure of internal colonialism is articulated with the centers of power of the Northern Hemisphere, whether they be universities, foundations, or international organizations. I refer to this crucial theme – the role of the intellectuals in the domination of empire – because I believe that it is our collective responsibility not to contribute to the reproduction of this domination. By participating in these forums and contributing to the exchange of ideas, we could be, unwittingly, providing the enemy with ammunition. And this enemy has multiple facets, both local and global, situated both in the small corners of "tiny power" in our universities and pauperized libraries and in the heights of prestige and privilege. It is from these "palaces" (the universities of the North) that, following [Gayatri Chakravorty] Spivak, dominant ideas emanate, and it is also there that the "think tanks" (suggestive of a war) of the imperial powers are located. The arboreal structure of internal–external colonialism has centers and subcenters, nodes and subnodes, which connect certain universities, disciplinary trends, and academic fashions of the North with their counterparts in the South.

Let us take the case of Duke University. Walter Mignolo, jointly appointed in romance studies and the Program in Literature, emigrated from Argentina in the 1980s and spent his Marxist youth in France and his postcolonial and culturalist maturity in the United States. At one point, Dr. Mignolo got the urge to praise me, perhaps putting in practice a saying we have in the south of Bolivia: "Praise the fool if you want to see [her] work more." Taking up my ideas about internal colonialism and the epistemology of oral history, he regurgitated them entangled in a discourse of alterity that was profoundly depoliticized.[15] Careful to avoid more polemical texts such as "Andean Colonial *Mestizaje*," he took on, out of context, ideas I had put forward in "The Epistemological and Theoretical Potential of Oral History," when the Andean Oral History Workshop was in its infancy and had not yet passed through the severe crisis that we are overcoming only today.[16] It was, therefore, an overly optimistic vision, which in many ways has been reworked in my most recent texts. But the North American academy does not follow the pace of our discussions; it does not interact with the Andean social sciences in any meaningful way (except by providing scholarships and invitations to seminars and symposia), and so Mignolo ignored these aspects of my thinking.

The fashion of oral history then spreads to the Universidad Andina Simon Bolivar in Quito, where the Department of Cultural Studies, led by Catherine Walsh, a disciple and friend of Mignolo's, offers a course of graduate study completely based in the logocentric and nominalist version of decolonization. Neologisms such as *decolonial*, *transmodernity*, and *eco-si-mía* proliferate, and such language entangles and paralyzes their objects of study: the indigenous and African-descended people with whom these academics believe they are in dialogue. But they also create a new academic canon, using a world of references and counter-references that establish hierarchies and adopt new gurus: Mignolo, Walsh, Enrique Dussel, Javier Sanjinés. Equipped with cultural and symbolic capital, thanks to the recognition and certification from the academic centers of the United States, this new structure of academic power is realized in practice through a network of guest lectureships and visiting professorships between universities and also through the flow – from the South to the North – of students of indigenous and African descent from Bolivia, Peru, and Ecuador, who are responsible for providing theoretical support for racialized and exoticized multiculturalism in the academies.

Therefore, instead of a "geopolitics of knowledge," I propose the task of undertaking a "political economy" of knowledge.[17] Not only because the "geopolitics of knowledge" in the decolonial sense is a notion that is not put into practice (it rather raises a contradiction through gestures that recolonize the imaginaries and minds of intellectuals of the South), but also because it is necessary to leave the sphere of the superstructures in order to analyze the economic strategies and material mechanisms that operate behind discourses. The postcolonial discourse of North America is not only an economy of ideas, but it is also an economy of salaries, perks, and privileges that certifies value through the granting of diplomas, scholarships, and master's degrees and through teaching and publishing opportunities. For obvious reasons and as the crisis deepens in public universities in Latin America, this kind of structure is well suited to the exercise of patronage as a mode of colonial domination. Through the game of who cites whom, hierarchies are structured, and we end up having to consume, in a regurgitated form, the very ideas regarding decolonization that we indigenous people and intellectuals of Bolivia, Peru, and Ecuador have produced independently. And this process began in the 1970s – the rarely quoted work of Pablo González Casanovas on "internal colonialism" was published in 1969 – when Mignolo and Quijano were still militants of a positivist Marxism and a linear vision of history.

Here is an anecdote. Some time ago I wrote a political critique of the Bolivian Left for a seminar organized by an academic foundation in Mexico. The article, titled "On the Problems of So-Called Leftists," was meant to criticize the way that the elites of the Marxist Left in Bolivia, because of their enlightenment and positivist vision, had overlooked the issue of Indian identity and the problems of decolonization, applying instead a reductionist and formulaic analysis that allowed them to facilely reproduce the cultural domination exercised by their class origin and by their proficiency in the legitimate language and Western thought. It was obvious that to do so, and to proclaim themselves spokespeople and interpreters of the demands of indigenous people, it was necessary to use obfuscating discourses. My article used the notion of "internal colonialism" extensively in order to analyze this superiority complex of middle-class intellectuals with respect to their indigenous peers and all the implications of this fact. The irony is that later the editors of an English-language journal suggested that I correct my sources. They indicated that I should cite Quijano's concept of "coloniality of knowledge" to make my text accessible to an audience completely unaware of the contributions of González Casanova and the Andean Oral History Workshop. I responded that I was not at fault if in 1983 Quijano had not read us – we had read him – and that my ideas about internal colonialism in terms of knowledge-power had come from a trajectory of thought that was entirely my own and had been illuminated by other readings, such as that of Maurice Halbwachs about collective memory, Frantz Fanon about the internalization of the enemy, Franco Ferraroti on life histories, and above all from the experience of having lived and participated in the reorganization of the Aymara movement and indigenous insurgency of the 1970s and 1980s.[18]

The vertical structure of this baseless pyramid that is produced by the academies of the North in their relations with the universities and intellectuals of the South expresses itself in multiple ways. For example, Quijano formulated the idea of coloniality of power in the 1990s, and Mignolo in turn created the notion of "colonial difference," thus reappropriating Quijano's ideas and adding nuances. It is through these processes that the notions of the "coloniality of knowledge" and the "geopolitics of knowledge" arose. In his book about the communal system, Félix Patzi in turn relies extensively on Quijano and Mignolo, ignoring the Kataristas' ideas regarding internal colonialism, which were formulated in the 1980s and had origins as far back as the late 1960s in the pioneering work of Fausto Reinaga.[19]

Ideas run, like rivers, from the south to the north and are transformed into tributaries in major waves of thought. But just as in the global market for material goods, ideas leave the country converted into raw material, which become regurgitated and jumbled in the final product. In this way, a canon is formed for a new field of social scientific discourse, postcolonial thinking. This canon makes visible certain themes and sources but leaves others in the shadows. Thus, Javier Sanjinés could write a whole book on *mestizaje* in Bolivia and completely disregard the entire Bolivian debate on this topic.[20] Thus we have cooptation and mimesis, the selective incorporation of ideas and selective approval of those that better nourish a fashionable, depoliticized, and comfortable multiculturalism that allows one to accumulate exotic masks in one's living room and to engage in absurd discussions about the future of public sector reforms. Can you believe that even the names of the ministries in the government reform of the first government of Sánchez de Lozada – including his symbolic adoption of the indigenous vice president Cárdenas – emerged from the offices of the United Nations Development Programme and the gatherings organized by Fernando Calderón [the Bolivian "decolonial" sociologist]?

I believe that the multiculturalism of Mignolo and company neutralizes the practices of decolonization by enthroning within the academy a limited and illusory discussion regarding modernity and decolonization. Without paying attention to the internal dynamics of the subalterns, cooptations of this type neutralize. They capture the energy and availability of indigenous intellectuals – brothers and sisters who may be tempted to play the ventriloquist of a convoluted conceptualization that deprives them of their roots and their dialogues with the mobilized masses.

The title of this paper is "*Ch'ixinakax utxiwa*." The world of *ch'ixi* also exists.[21] Personally, I don't consider myself *q'ara* (culturally stripped and usurped by others), because I recognize my fully double origin, Aymara and European, and because I live from my own efforts. Because of this, I consider myself *ch'ixi* and consider it the most appropriate translation of the motley mix that we, who are called *mestizas* and *mestizos*, are. The word *ch'ixi* has many connotations: it is a color that is the product of juxtaposition, in small points or spots, of opposed or contrasting colors: black and white, red and green, and so on. It is this heather gray that comes from the imperceptible mixing of black and white, which are confused by perception, without ever being completely mixed. The notion of *ch'ixi*, like many others (*allqa*, *ayni*), reflects the Aymara idea of something that is and is not at the same time. It is the logic of the included third. A *ch'ixi* color gray is white but is not white at the same time; it is both white and its opposite, black. The *ch'ixi* stone, therefore, is hidden in the bosom of mythical animals like the serpent, the lizard, the spider, or the frog; *ch'ixi* animals belong to time immemorial, to *jaya mara*, *aymara*, to times of differentiation, when animals spoke with humans. The potential of undifferentiation is what joins opposites. And so as *allqamari* combines black and white in symmetrical perfection, *ch'ixi* combines the Indian world and its opposite without ever mixing them. But *ch'ixi*'s heteronomy also alludes in turn to the idea of muddling, to a loss of sustenance and energy. *Ch'ixi* is firewood that burns very fast, that which is feeble and intermingled. It parallels, then, this fashionable notion of cultural hybridity lite conforming to contemporary cultural domination.

The notion of hybridity proposed by Néstor García Canclini is a genetic metaphor that connotes infertility.[22] Yet, hybridity assumes the possibility that from the mixture of two different beings a third completely new one can emerge, a third race or social group with the capacity to merge the features of its ancestors in a harmonic and as yet unknown blend. But the mule is a hybrid that cannot reproduce. The notion of *ch'ixi*, on the contrary, amounts to the "motley" [*abigarrada*] society of René Zavaleta and expresses the parallel coexistence of multiple cultural differences that do not extinguish but instead antagonize and complement each other. Each one reproduces itself from the depths of the past and relates to others in a contentious way.

The possibility of a profound cultural reform in our society depends on the decolonization of our gestures and acts and the language with which we name the world. The reappropriation of bilingualism as a decolonizing practice will allow for the creation of a "we" as producers of knowledge and interlocutors who can have discussions as equals with other centers of thought and currents in the academies of our region and also of the world. The metaphor of *ch'ixi* assumes a double and contentious ancestry, one that is denied by the processes of acculturation and the "colonization of the imaginary" but one that is also potentially harmonious and free if we liberate our half-Indian ancestry and develop dialogical forms for the construction of knowledges.

The metaphor of hybridity suggests that we can "enter and leave modernity," as if it were a stadium or a theater, instead of a constructive process – simultaneously objective and subjective – of habits, gestures, modes of interaction, and ideas about the world. The Indian commitment to modernity centers itself on a notion of citizenship that does not look for homogeneity but rather for difference. But at the same time, as a project in pursuit of hegemony, it has the ability to translate, in practical terms, the fields of politics and of the state, supposing a capacity to organize society in our image and likeness, to build a lasting cultural fabric, and to set legitimate and stable norms of coexistence. This implies the construction of a homeland for everyone. Eduardo Nina Qhispi, linked to the *movimiento de caciques-apoderados* from the 1920s and 1930s, formulated his utopia of the "reinvention of Bolivia" in a context of the colonial deafness of the oligarchical elites and of ready warriors, who, on the internal front, dismantled the leadership of the communities. In this desirable society, *mestizos* and Indians could live together on equal terms, by adopting, from the beginning, legitimate modes of coexistence based in reciprocity, redistribution, and authority as a service. Further, in this society the Indians would expand and adopt their culturally patterned ideas of democratic coexistence and good government and admit new forms of community and mixed identities, or *ch'ixi*, and thus enter into a creative dialogue in a process of exchanging knowledges, aesthetics, and ethics.

In this vein, the notion of identity as territory is unique to men, and the forms of organization that were adopted by the indigenous people of Bolivia are still marked by the colonial seal of the exclusion of women. It is a project of reinvention in Bolivia that will overcome the official multiculturalism that confines and stereotypes us and that would also return us to the macho logocentrism that draws maps and establishes belonging. The notion of the identity of women, however, is similar to a fabric. Far from establishing the property and the jurisdiction of the authority of the nation – or the people, the autonomous indigenous – the feminine practice weaves the fabric of the intercultural through women's practices as producers, merchants, weavers, ritualists, and creators of languages and symbols capable of seducing the "other" and establishing pacts of reciprocity and coexistence among different groups. This seductive labor, elaborated by and shared among women, allows for the complementing of the territorial homeland with a dynamic cultural fabric that reproduces itself and spreads until it reaches the mixed and frontier areas – the *ch'ixi* areas – and there contributes its vision of personal responsibility, privacy, and individual rights associated with citizenship. The modernity that emerges from these motley relations and complex and mixed languages – Gamaliel Churata called them "a language with a homeland"[23] – is what builds the Indian hegemony to be realized in spaces that were created by the cultural invader: the market, the state, the union. In doing so, we create our own project of modernity, a more organic one than that imposed by the elites, who live through ventriloquizing concepts and theories and through academic currents and visions of the world copied from the North or tributaries from the centers of hegemonic power.

Decolonizing thinking will allow us to create a different Bolivia that is genuinely multicultural and decolonized, and part of the affirmation of this is our bilingualism, multicolored and *ch'ixi*, which projects itself as culture, theory, epistemology, and state policy and also in new definitions of well-being and development. The challenge of this new autonomy is in constructing South–South links that will allow us to break the baseless pyramids of the politics and academies of the North and that will enable us to make our own science, in a dialogue among ourselves and with the sciences from our neighboring countries, by affirming our bonds with theoretical currents of Asia and Africa – that is, to confront the hegemonic projects of the North with the renewed strength of our ancestral convictions.

Notes

The abridged English edition of Felipe Guaman Poma de Ayala's *First New Chronicle and Good Government* has been quoted where possible; any text which was not included in the English edition has been translated by Molly Geidel.

Introduction: The Silvia Rivera Cusicanqui Principle: The Rebellion of Thought

1 See Vladimir Lenin, *What is to be Done? Burning Questions of Our Movement* (Moscow: Original Progress Publishers Moscow, 2017), 110. Here we preserve the version of Lenin's words closer to the Spanish translation of the passage Rivera Cusicanqui remembers rather than using one of the more standard English translations.

2 Silvia Rivera Cusicanqui, *Oppressed but not Defeated: Peasant Struggles Among the Aymara and Quechwa in Bolivia, 1900–1980* (Geneva: United Nations Research Institute for Social Development, 1987).

3 Gustavo Cruz, "Poder indio y poder negro: recepciones del pensamiento negro en Fausto Reinaga" ("Indian

Power and Black Power: The Reception of Black Thought in Fausto Reinaga"), *Iconos*. 51 (Jan./Feb. 2015): 39.

4 Ibid., 45.

5 Silvia Rivera Cusicanqui, *Violencias (re)encubiertas en Bolivia ((Re)hidden Violences in Bolivia)* (La Paz: La Mirada Salvaje, 2010), 232.

6 The basic unit of Andean social organization; a territory-based grouping that unites indigenous people from various lineages and networks through ties of blood, affinity, and territory, as well as symbolic referents.

7 As Rivera Cusicanqui explains, while the colonial society is strengthened, the women who abandoned "their indigenous garments to adopt the Spanish *pollera* and shawl were unknowingly creating the traits of identification that later would distinguish 'the chola' from other sectors of urban society" (Rivera Cusicanqui, *Violencias (re)encubiertas en Bolivia*, 75). For a deeper understanding, see Rossana Barragán's text "Entre polleras, lliqllas y ñañacas. los mestizos y la emergencia de la tercera república" ("Between Chicken Farmers, *lliqllas*, and *ñañacas*. Mestizos and the Emergence of the Third Republic"), in *Etnicidad, economía y simbolismo en los Andes*, vol. 2, *Congreso Internacional de Etnohistoria, Coroico* (*Ethnicity, Economy, and Symbolism in the Andes*, vol. 2, *International Ethnohistorical Conference, Coroico*), ed. Silvia Arze et al. (La Paz: hisbol-IFEA-SBH/ASUR, 1992).

8 Silvia Rivera Cusicanqui, *Bircholas: trabajo de mujeres. Explotación capitalista y opresión colonial entre las migrantes aymaras de La Paz y El Alto (Bircholas: Women's Work. Capitalist Exploitation and Colonial Oppression between Aymara Migrants in La Paz and El Alto)* (La Paz: Editorial Mama Huaco, 2002).

9 Silvia Rivera Cusicanqui, *Las fronteras de la coca: epistemologías coloniales y circuitos alternativos de la hoja de coca. El caso de la frontera boliviano–argentina (Coca Frontiers: Colonial Epistemologies and Alternative*

Circuits of the Coca Leaf. The Case of the Bolivia–Argentina Border) (La Paz: IDIS, 2003).

10 Silvia Rivera Cusicanqui, *Mito y desarrollo en Bolivia. El giro colonial del gobierno del MAS* (*Myth and Development in Bolivia. The Colonial Turn of the MAS Government*) (La Paz: Plural-Piedra Rota, 2015).

11 Silvia Rivera Cusicanqui and Verónica Gago, "Orgullo de ser mestiza" ("*Mestiza* Pride"), *Las/12*, diario *Página/12* (July 30, 2010), *https://www.pagina12.com.ar/diario/suplementos/las12/13-5889-2010-07-30.html*.

12 Silvia Rivera Cusicanqui and Rossana Barragán (eds.), *Debates post coloniales. Una introducción a los estudios de la subalternidad* (*Postcolonial Debates. An Introduction to Subaltern Studies*) (La Paz: Historia-Sephis-Aruwiyiri, 1997).

13 Silvia Rivera Cusicanqui, *Sociología de la imagen. Miradas ch'ixi desde la historia andina* (*Sociology of the Image. Ch'ixi Gazes from Andean History*) (Buenos Aires: Tinta Limón, 2015).

14 All quotations not otherwise identified (as here) are from conversations and notes from a seminar Rivera Cusicanqui gave in Buenos Aires in 2016, co-organized by three public universities (UNSAM, UBA, and UNTREF).

15 Her works are the video docufiction *Khunuskiw, recuerdos del porvenir* (*Khunuskiw, Memories of the Future*) (La Paz, 1993) and the 16mm fictional short *Sueño en el cuarto rojo* (*Dream in the Red Room*) (La Paz, 2000). More recently, we can find the current of protest documentary and cultural memory in the two videos that annex *Las fronteras de la coca: junio 2001*, titled *La retirada de los Yungas* (*Retreat of the Yungas*) and *Viaje a la frontera del sur* (*Travel to the Southern Border*) (Jakima Productions, 2003). With codirector Marco Arnéz she also made the shorts *Fin de fiesta* (*End of the Fiesta*) and *Sumaj qhaniri, chuyma manqharu* (*You Who Illuminate the Dark Center of My Heart*).

16 Rivera Cusicanqui and El Colectivo 2, *Principio Potosí*

Reverso (*The Reverse Potosí Principle*) (Madrid: Museo Reina Sofía, 2010).

17 Interview with author, Buenos Aires, 2016.

18 Ibid.

19 See René Zavaleta Mercado, "Las masas en Noviembre" ("The Masses of November"), in *Bolivia hoy* (*Bolivia Today*), ed. René Zavaleta Mercado (Mexico City: Siglo XXI, 1983).

20 Rivera Cusicanqui, this volume, p. 65.

21 Ibid., p. 65.

22 Ibid, p. 66.

23 See note 5 above.

24 Square of cloth folded ingeniously to carry a baby on one's back, traditionally used by Andean indigenous women. – Trans.

25 Rivera Cusicanqui and Gago, "Orgullo de ser mestiza."

26 Aymara-inflected Spanish; see discussion on p. xxvi.

27 Rivera Cusicanqui and Gago, "Orgullo de ser mestiza."

28 Silvia Rivera Cusicanqui, *Un mundo ch'ixi es posible: ensayos desde un presente en crisis* (*A Ch'ixi World is Possible: Essays from the Present Crisis*) (Buenos Aires: Tinta Limón, 2018).

Chapter 1 Another Bicentennial

1 See Mario T. Soria, *Teatro boliviano en el siglo XX* (*Bolivian Theater in the Twentieth Century*) (La Paz: Editorial Casa Municipal de la Cultura Franz Tamayo, 1980).

2 These themes are being explored in ongoing research by Pablo Mamani and Sinclair Thomson about the memory and present-day ideological repercussions of the rebellion cycle of Tupaq Katari (personal communication, July 14, 2008).

3 Sinclair Thomson, *We Alone Will Rule: Native Andean*

Politics in the Age of Insurgency (Madison: University of Wisconsin Press, 2002).

4 Ibid., 18–21.

5 A Quechua nobleman who chronicled the Spanish conquest of the Andes. See "Sociology of the Image" in this volume.

6 Felipe Guaman Poma de Ayala, Felipe, *First New Chronicle and Good Government* (abridged), trans. David Frye (Indianapolis: Hackett, 2006), 392.

7 Ibid., 453.

8 Ibid., 278.

Chapter 2 Sociology of the Image: A View from Colonial Andean History

1 This idea of the world upside down emerges again in the work of a Chuquisacan painter from the mid-nineteenth century who, in his precarious political life as a prisoner and a deportee, came to know the most remote areas of the country and to live together with barely known indigenous populations, like the Bororos in the Iténez or the Chacobos and Moxeños on the eastern plains. For him, the world upside down alluded to the government of the republic in the hands of beasts who yoked workers to the plow of the oxen ("Secuencias iconográficas en Melchor María Mercado" ("Iconographic Sequences in Melchor María Mercado"), in *El Siglo XIX. Bolivia y América Latina* (*The Nineteenth Century. Bolivia and Latin America*), ed. Rossana Barragán, Seemin Quayum, and Magdalena Cajías [La Paz: IFEA-Historias, 1997]). Certainly this painter, Melchor María Mercado, did not know the work of Guaman Poma, which was discovered in a Copenhagen library at the beginning of the last century. This idea must have arrived to him through oral tradition, perhaps grounded in the indigenous notion

of *Pachakuti*, the reversal or overturning of time/space, which inaugurates long cycles of catastrophe or renewal of the cosmos.

2 Felipe Guaman Poma de Ayala (Waman Puma), *El primer nueva corónica y buen gobierno (First New Chronicle and Good Government)*, ed. Rolena Adorno, John Murra, and Jorge Urioste (Mexico City: Siglo XXI, 1980), 1027.

3 Ibid.

4 Felipe Guaman Poma de Ayala, *First New Chronicle and Good Government* (abridged), trans. David Frye (Indianapolis: Hackett, 2006), 78.

5 Ibid.

6 Guaman Poma, *El primer nueva corónica*, 195.

7 Jan Szeminski, *La utopía tupamarista (The Tupamarist Utopia)* (Lima: PUCP, 1984).

8 Candia appeared in the Andes in 1527, sent by Francisco Pizarro, who, upon receiving Candia's news, returned to Spain to form a military expedition, assured of the existence of precious metals in the Andean empire.

9 See p. 45 below.

10 Guaman Poma, *First New Chronicle*, 110.

11 Ibid., 156.

12 This text appears within the space of Guaman Poma's drawing of the assassination of Tupaq Amaru

13 Walter Benjamin, "Theses on the Philosophy of History," in *Illuminations*, ed. Hannah Arendt (New York: Verso, 1971), 280.

14 Guaman Poma, *El primer nueva corónica*, 210.

15 Ibid., 213.

16 Ibid., 214.

17 Ibid., 217.

18 Ibid., 219.

19 Ibid., 221.

20 Ibid., 223.

21 Ibid., 225.

22 Ibid., 227.

23 Ibid., 229.

24 Ibid., 231.
25 Ibid., 233.
26 Ibid., 190.
27 Guaman Poma, *First New Chronicle*, 209–10.
28 Guaman Poma, *El primer nueva corónica*, 611.
29 Ibid., 468.
30 Ibid., 383.

Chapter 3 *Ch'ixinakax utxiwa*: A Reflection on the Practices and Discourses of Decolonization

1 Sinclair Thomson, *We Alone Will Rule: Native Andean Politics in the Age of Insurgency* (Madison: University of Wisconsin Press, 2002).
2 Paulina Numhauser, *Mujeres indias y señores de la coca. Potosí y Cuzco en el siglo XVI* (*Indian Women and the Men of Coca. Potosí and Cuzco in the Sixteenth Century*) (Madrid: Ediciones Cátedra, 2005).
3 These were the heroes and martyrs of indigenous resistance against colonialism. Tomás Katari was an Aymara appointed as cacique to the indigenous people of Potosí, Bolivia, by the Spanish crown. He advocated for peaceful resistance against the Spanish that could lead to a series of reforms and the establishment of a utopic Aymara society. Katari was eventually executed for his beliefs and for the actions of his followers. Tupaq Amaru II (born José Gabriel Condorcanqui) was the leader of the indigenous/*mestizo* uprising against the Bourbon reforms of the Spanish in 1780 in and around Cuzco, Peru (he was executed shortly thereafter). By early 1781 news of Tupaq Amaru's uprising had spread to what is now Bolivia, where Julian Apasa Nina (taking the name Tupaq Katari in honor of Tomás Katari and Tupaq Amaru II) along with his wife, Bartolina Sisa, and Tupaq

Amaru's brother, Diego, laid siege to the city of La Paz for nearly six months (after which he, too, was captured and executed). For a wonderful account of the scope and context of these uprisings, see Thomson, *We Alone Will Rule*. For an account of how these uprisings continue to influence contemporary Andean movements, see Forrest Hylton and Sinclair Thomson, *Revolutionary Horizons: Past and Present in Bolivian Politics* (New York: Verso, 2007). – Ed.

4　Partha　Chatterjee,　*Our　Modernity*　(Amsterdam/ Rotterdam/Dakar: SEPHIS/CODESRIA, 1997).

5　Ernst Bloch, *Principle of Hope*, 3 vols., trans. Neville Plaice, Stephen Plaice, and Paul Knight (Boston: MIT Press, 1995); and Bloch, "Nonsynchronism and the Obligation to Its Dialectics," trans. Mark Ritter, *New German Critique*, no. 11 (1977): 22–38.

6　Walter Benjamin, "Theses on the Philosophy of History," in *Illuminations* (New York: Schocken, 1969), 253–64.

7　Silvia Rivera Cusicanqui, "Rebelión e ideologia" ("Rebellion and Ideology"), *Historia Boliviana* 2 (1981): n.p.

8　Silvia Rivera Cusicanqui, *Oppressed but Not Defeated: Peasant Struggles among the Aymara and Qhechwa in Bolivia, 1900–1980* (Geneva: United Nations Research Institute for Social Development, 1987).

9　Ranajit Guha, "The Prose of Counter-Insurgency," in *Selected Subaltern Studies*, ed. Ranajit Guha and Gayatri Chakravorty Spivak (Oxford: Oxford University Press, 1988), 12–40.

10　Edward Said, *Orientalism* (New York: Vintage, 1979).

11　Rossana Barragán, "Entre polleras, lliqllas y ñañacas. Los mestizos y la emergencia de la tercera república" ("Between Chicken Farmers, *lliqllas* and *ñañacas*. The Mestizos and the Emergence of the Third Republic") in *Etnicidad, economía y simbolismo en los Andes*, vol. 2, *Congreso Internacional de Etnohistoria, Coroico* (*Ethnicity, Economy, and Symbolism in the Andes*, vol. 2, *International Ethnohistorical Conference, Coroico*), ed. Silvia Arze et al. (La Paz: Hisbol-IFEA-SBH/ASUR, 1992).

12 *Zero coca* was a coca eradication program implemented under President Hugo Banzer Suárez.

13 This lecture was given at a time when a rupture with the crisis of the state – such as the one produced on December 18, 2005, which ended with the triumph of Evo Morales's MAS [Movimiento al Socialismo] – and the formation of the first modern government in the Americas in the hands of an indigenous person was not even thought possible.

14 Pablo González Casanovas, *Sociología de la explotación* (*The Sociology of Exploitation*) (Mexico City: Grijalbo, 1969). Although there is no existing translation of González Casanovas's book into English, an article in which he explores similar themes was published in English as "Internal Colonialism and National Development," *Studies in Comparative International Development* 1, no. 4 (1965): 27–37.

15 Walter Mignolo, "El potencial epistemológico de la historia oral: algunas contribuciones de Silvia Rivera Cusicanqui" ("The Epistemological Potential of Oral History: Some Contributions by Silvia Rivera Cusicanqui"), in *Estudios e outras práticas intelectuales Latinamericanas en cultura e poder* (*Studies and Other Latin American Intellectual Practices in Culture and Power*), ed. Daniel Mato (Caracas: CLASCO, 2002), 201–12.

16 Silvia Rivera Cusicanqui, "El potencial epistemologico y teórico de la historia oral: de la logica instrumental a la descolonización de la historia" ("The Epistemological and Theoretical Potential of Oral History: From Instrumental Logic to the Decolonization of History"), *Temas Sociales* 11 (1989): 49–75.

17 Walter Mignolo, "The Geopolitics of Knowledge and the Colonial Difference," *South Atlantic Quarterly* 101, no. 1 (2002): 57–96.

18 See Maurice Halbwachs, *On Collective Memory*, ed. and

trans. Lewis A. Coser (Chicago: University of Chicago Press, 1992); Frantz Fanon, *The Wretched of the Earth*, trans. Richard Philcox (New York: Grove Press, 2004); and Franco Ferraroti, *Histoire et histoires de vie (History and Histories of Life)* (Paris: Presses Universitaires de France, 1982).

19 See Félix Patzi, *Sistema comunal. Una alternativa al sistema liberal (The Communal System. An Alternative to the Liberal System)* (La Paz: CEEA, 2004); and Fausto Reinaga, *La revolución India (The Indian Revolution)* (La Paz: Ediciones PIB, 1969).

20 Javier Sanjinés, *Mestizaje Upside-Down: Aesthetic Politics in Modern Bolivia* (Pittsburgh, PA: University of Pittsburgh Press, 2004).

21 The next section of this paper was developed by Rivera Cusicanqui from a conference presentation that she gave in Aymara. The lack of translation for Aymara words in the following paragraphs is accounted for by the fact that Rivera Cusicanqui is attempting to give non-Aymara-speakers a summary of the concepts that she develops. – Trans.

22 Néstor García Canclini, *Hybrid Cultures: Strategies for Entering and Leaving Modernity*, trans. Christopher Chiappari and Silvia L. López (Minneapolis: University of Minnesota Press, 1995).

23 Gamaliel Churata, *El pez de Oro (The Golden Fish)* (Cochabamba: Editorial Canata, 1957), 14.

Bibliography

Adorno, Rolena, "Paradigms Lost: A Peruvian Indian Surveys Spanish Colonial Society," *Studies in the Anthropology of Visual Communication 5*, no. 2 (1979): 78–96.

Barragán, Rossana, "Entre polleras, lliqllas y ñañacas. Los mestizos y la emergencia de la tercera república," in *Etnicidad, economía y simbolismo en los Andes*, vol. 2, *Congreso Internacional de Etnohistoria, Coroico*, ed. Silvia Arze et al. La Paz: Hisbol-IFEA-SBH/ASUR, 1992.

Benjamin, Walter, "Theses on the Philosophy of History," in *Illuminations*, ed. Hannah Arendt. New York: Verso, 1971.

Bloch, Ernst, "Nonsynchronism and the Obligation to Its Dialectics," trans. Mark Ritter, *New German Critique*, no. 11 (1977): 22–38.

Chatterjee, Partha, *Our Modernity*. Amsterdam/Rotterdam/Dakar: SEPHIS/CODESRIA, 1997.

Churata, Gamaliel, *El pez de plata. Recuerdos del laykakuy*. La Paz: s.p.e., 1950.

Fabian, Johanes, *Time and the Other: How Anthropology Makes Its Object*. New York: Columbia University Press, 1982.

Ferraroti, Franco, *Histoire et histoires de vie*. Paris: Presses Universitaires de France, 1982.

Foucault, Michel, *The Archaeology of Knowledge*, trans. A.M. Sheridan Smith. London: Routledge, 1989.

García Canclini, Néstor, *Hybrid Cultures: Strategies for Entering and Leaving Modernity*, trans. Christopher L. Chiappari and Silvia L. López. Minneapolis: University of Minnesota Press, 1995.

González Casanova, Pablo, *Sociología de la explotación*. Mexico City: Grijalbo, 1969.

Guaman Poma de Ayala, Felipe (Waman Puma), *El primer nueva corónica y buen gobierno*, ed. Rolena Adorno, John Murra, and Jorge Urioste Mexico City: Siglo XXI, 1980.

Guaman Poma de Ayala, Felipe, *First New Chronicle and Good Government* (abridged), trans. David Frye. Indianapolis: Hackett, 2006.

Guha, Ranajit, "The Prose of Counter-Insurgency," in *Selected Subaltern Studies*, ed. Ranajit Guha and Gayatri Chakravorty Spivak. Oxford: Oxford University Press, 1988.

Halbwachs, Maurice, *On Collective Memory*, ed. and trans. Lewis A. Coser. Chicago: University of Chicago Press, 1992.

Kymlica, Will, *Multicultural Citizenship: A Liberal Theory of Minority Rights*. Oxford: Clarendon Press, 1995.

Mamani Condori, Carlos, *Taraqu 1866–1935. Masacre, guerra y "renovación" en la biografía de Eduardo L. Nina Qhispi*. La Paz: Aruwiyiri, 1991.

Mignolo, Walter, "The Geopolitics of Knowledge and the Colonial Difference," *South Atlantic Quarterly* 101, no. 1 (2002): 57–96.

Numhauser, Paulina, *Mujeres indias y señores de la coca. Potosí y Cuzco en el siglo XVI*. Madrid: Ediciones Cátedra, 2005.

Patzi, Félix, *Sistema comunal. Una alternativa al Sistema liberal*. La Paz: CEEA, 2004.

Rivera Cusicanqui, Silvia, "Rebelión e ideología," *Historia Boliviana* 2 (1981): n.p.

Rivera Cusicanqui, Silvia, "Mestizaje colonial andino. Una hipótesis de trabajo", in Silvia Rivera Cusicanqui and Raúl Barrios, *Violencias encubiertas en Bolivia*, vol. 1, *Cultura y política*, ed. Xavier Albó. La Paz: CIPCA-Aruwiyiri, 1993.

Rivera Cusicanqui, Silvia, "Secuencias iconográficas en Melchor María Mercado," in *El Siglo XIX. Bolivia y América Latina*, ed. Rossana Barragán, Seemin Quayum, and Magdalena Cajías. La Paz: IFEA-Historias, 1997.

Rivera Cusicanqui, Silvia, "Mirando los problemas de las llamadas izquierdas", in *Las izquierdas en México y América Latina. Desafíos, peligros y posibilidades*. Mexico City: Fundación Heberto Castillo Martínez, A.C., 2004.

Rivera Cusicanqui, Silvia, "The Ch'ixi Identity of a Mestizo: Regarding an Anarchist Manifesto of 1929," trans. Molly Geidel, in *No Gods, No Masters, No Peripheries: Global Anarchisms*, ed. Barry Maxwell and Raymond Craib. Oakland, CA: PM Press, 2015.

Said, Edward W., *Orientalism*. New York: Pantheon, 1978.

Sanjinés, Javier, *El espejismo del mestizaje*. La Paz: IFEA, Embajada de Francia y PIEB, 2005.

Spivak, Gayatri Chakravorty, *In Other Worlds: Essays in Cultural Politics*. New York/London: Routledge, 1987.

Taller de Historia Oral Andina, *El indio Santos Marka T'ula, cacique principal de los ayllus de Qallapa y apoderado general de las comunidades originarias de la República*. La Paz: THOA-UMSA, 1984.

Taller de Historia Oral Andina, *Mujer y resistencia comunaria: historia y memoria*. La Paz: HISBOL, 1986.

Thomson, Sinclair, *We Alone Will Rule: Native Andean Politics in the Age of Insurgency*. Madison: University of Wisconsin Press, 2002.

Walsh, Catherine, Freya Schiwy, and Sara Castro Gómez (eds.), *Indisciplinar las ciencias sociales. Geopolíticas del conocimiento y colonialidad del poder. Perspectivas desde lo andino*. Quito: Abya-Yala/UASB, 2002.

Index